The Key to Confidence

where to go when you feel you're not enough

by Amber Albee Swenson

Published by Straight Talk Books
P.O. Box 301, Milwaukee, WI 53201
800.661.3311 • timeofgrace.org

Printed in the United States of America

ISBN: 978-1-965694-14-5

Contents

Preface

This book is *not* about becoming confident in yourself. If it was, I would not have been the one to write it. It isn't a self-help or "take these three steps and ta-da you can do it" book. It's a book about identity and prayer. When you know whose you are and when you understand the unlimited power God has—and that he works on your behalf—you can be the warrior in God's kingdom you were meant to be. Not because you are so great or talented but because God is great and can do infinitely more than you ever could.

It still baffles me that God in his infinite wisdom decides to work through frail, weak, and sometimes utterly ridiculous people. But he does.

If I've learned anything in the last several years, it's that it's never about me. Working in God's kingdom is about Christ today and every day, about leaning on him for help and strength, and about going to him in prayer. That's where we get our confidence and our hope. None of us will ever be enough, but God is more than enough for all of us.

—Amber

CHAPTER 1

Confident You Can Get Past Your Past

I did not title this chapter flippantly. I can ruminate, overthink, replay, and get stuck with the best of ruminators, overthinkers, and those who are stuck.

Almost all of us have things in our past we wish weren't part of our story: the reckless decisions of youth, the hurtful words that burrowed their way into our identities or equally cruel words we said that burrowed their way into someone else's, the thoughtless words and actions of someone we trusted who let us down, the people we let down who trusted us.

If willing yourself or someone else whole and healed was all it took, emotional scars wouldn't paralyze and triggers wouldn't have the power to take you back to the hurt you felt or the pain you've caused. If you've done life with the "just get over it" mentality, you may have found burying the pain is like pushing a floatie underwater. It pops back to the surface at the most inconvenient times.

That's why it's important to reconcile the past. To *reconcile* is "to coexist in harmony; make compatible; settle." Reconciling doesn't mean the hurt goes away. It just means that like Joseph (whose life is chronicled in chapters 37–50 in the book of Genesis), you will be able to declare what was meant to harm you has indeed been used for good. It means you haven't let bitterness take root, and you've worked to forgive if necessary or give it over to God to bring something good from the pain.

Let me be clear. "Used for good" does not mean what happened was good. God using the bad for good is not an excuse for bad behavior, thoughtless actions, or treating people as less than the children of God that they are. It just means you serve a good God who takes the worst and uses it in ways that are often mysterious to you in the moment but powerful in hindsight.

In the book of Ruth in the Old Testament, we are introduced to Naomi. For Naomi, the worst began with a famine that led to an out-of-country move. There her husband died. Her two sons married, but after ten years, both of them died as well. Any one of those things is life changing and traumatic. But those four things compounded led Naomi to say:

> **"Do not call me Naomi. . . . Call me Mara (which means bitter), because the Almighty has made my life very bitter. I went away full, but the Lord has brought me back empty. Why call me Naomi? For**

the Lord has afflicted me; the Almighty has brought misfortune upon me." (1:20,21)

In the thick of Naomi's pain, she couldn't see or feel or imagine anything good coming from the circumstances. She understood God controlled life and death. By default, that meant he allowed her loved ones to be taken from her, and that seemed an inconceivable cruelty.

God working for good included Naomi bringing a widowed foreigner—her daughter-in-law Ruth—back to Israel. Ruth provided for Naomi by going to the fields and picking up leftover grain. And there in Israel a distant relative of Naomi's became their redeemer.

The note in my study Bible says, "The redeemer was a kind of guardian who gave legal and financial support to less-well-off relatives, especially by regaining a lost inheritance or by redeeming someone from slavery."[1]

Ruth married this godly redeemer (named Boaz), and together they were the great-grandparents of King David. Naomi's heartbreak turned to joy as she watched it all unfold.

Don't miss how all this came about. The famine led Naomi to Ruth. The death of her loved ones brought Naomi and Ruth to Boaz and the line of the Savior.

Life in a sin-filled world means that struggles will happen. Maybe not a famine. Maybe for you it's losing a relationship or a job or a position of authority.

Consider the hardships you've endured in the past. Think about the closed doors, the things that didn't turn out, the relationships that ended. At the time the pain may have seemed considerable, overwhelming even. But can you see how God worked in some way despite the pain? Maybe you can't see it yet. Maybe the pain is still fresh, and the tears haven't dried. Maybe it's been five years, and you really wonder if any good is possible. It is.

I loved my father-in-law. When my husband, Steve, and I planted a garden in my father-in-law's backyard, he kept it weed free. We didn't realize he had been weeding it until the year he wasn't around to do it.

My children were five, three, and six months old when he died. We suddenly had a new set of responsibilities caring for Steve's mom's house and yard. I didn't see how good could come from my father-in-law's absence. And I couldn't fathom having a fourth child without him around to help.

My desire was for my father-in-law to live a long life and help us raise our family. But God desired that I learn to love and support a widow, someone I didn't always appreciate or understand while my father-in-law was alive. And God wanted me to learn to rely on him and the strength he would provide, not anyone else.

All these years later, I see how God took something painful and hard and blessed my mother-in-law and me with a beautiful relationship, gave me greater empathy, and even blessed our family financially. Most years my mother-in-law gave us a check at the end of the year in appreciation for all the help we provided. We decided early on to use that money for family vacations that we otherwise couldn't afford. Those vacations were some of my children's fondest memories growing up.

It's so easy to get stuck in the past, and if you're not careful, you'll live a life of longing and regret, rather than looking forward to what God has in store for you in the future.

It's so easy to get stuck in the past.

Samuel was Israel's last prophet before it became a monarchy. Samuel anointed Saul king and then watched King Saul's lackluster obedience to God.

Finally, God had enough. When Saul failed to follow directions, Samuel told Saul, **"You have rejected the word of the Lord, and the Lord has rejected you as king over Israel!"** (1 Samuel 15:26).

Here's what happened next:

> **Then Samuel left for Ramah, but Saul went up to his home in Gibeah of Saul. Until the day Samuel died, he did not go to see Saul again, though Samuel mourned for him. And the Lord regretted that he had made Saul king over Israel.**
>
> **The Lord said to Samuel, "How long will you mourn for Saul, since I have rejected him as king over Israel? Fill your horn with oil and be on your way; I am sending you to Jesse of Bethlehem. I have chosen one of his sons to be king."** (1 Samuel 15:34–16:1)

Samuel could feel bad, and he could mourn, but it wasn't going to change the situation. God didn't want that for Samuel. And he doesn't want that for you. God wanted and needed Samuel to move from the past to the present and then to the future. At some point, and hopefully sooner rather than later, you and I have to move forward too.

If you've said goodbye to someone you love, you know this. As much as you want time to stop, or preferably even go back, that isn't going to happen. People still get hungry. Bills still need to be paid. The grass keeps growing. No one else seems phased by the time warp loss brings. And so you go on.

The Israelites had been enslaved in Egypt for four hundred years. Through a series of miracles, God brought them out of Egypt, and Moses led them into the desert. Pharaoh decided that he had made a terrible mistake letting the people go, so he gathered his chariots and went after the Israelites. The people of Israel found themselves in the desert with the Red Sea in front of them and Pharaoh's army behind. What a dilemma!

When the people complained that it must have been because there were no graves in Egypt that Moses brought them to the desert, Moses answered,

> **"Do not be afraid. Stand firm and you will see the deliverance the Lord will bring you today. The Egyptians you see today you will never see again. The Lord will fight for you; you need only to be still."**

Then the Lord said to Moses, "Why are you crying out to me? Tell the Israelites to move on. Raise your staff and stretch out your hand over the sea to divide the water so that the Israelites can go through the sea on dry ground." (Exodus 14:13-16)

Did you notice God's command? Get moving!

The Israelites could have taken this time to think about the past and the four hundred long years of slavery, about a freedom they had never known. They could have commiserated about their treatment and the cruelty of the Egyptians who mercilessly killed their baby boys. They could have sat down and wept or rolled in a ball or thrown up their hands saying, "It's too much. We can't take anymore!"

But God wanted them to move because he was about to destroy the people who had held them captive. And he would show Israel how far he would go to work on their behalf—even opening up a sea—so they could distance themselves from their enemies.

For a time, it can feel safe to stay put and build walls. You can set each brick carefully in place and make the walls high and wide, protecting your heart to make sure nothing hurts you that way again. Every time you feel emotions you don't want to feel, you add layers to the wall. You keep people out. You are fine; everything is fine; it's all good.

And though it is one way to deal, let me warn you: The walls that keep hurt out also keep the pain in. And trying to appear strong while hiding behind walls is exhausting.

God has put amazing women in my life who have taught me the importance of being a woman who controls my mouth. I've learned not to say something if it isn't my story to tell. I've worked hard to be the trustworthy friend, the vault, who holds others' secrets and prays but doesn't let others know what I know. Unfortunately, I have also at times trusted the wrong people. All those things, along with my own insecurities, have made it hard for me to let people in.

A few months ago, I made my way through the apostle Paul's letters. His transparency was off the charts. He named names. He told it like it was. When it was bad, he wrote that it was bad. **"We do not want you to be uninformed, brothers and sisters, about the troubles we experienced in the province of Asia. We were under great pressure, far beyond our ability to endure, so that we despaired of life itself"** (2 Corinthians 1:8).

Our social media culture likes to make it look like everything is under control, and people don't want to hear how much work you've done to make something happen. To some, that is looking for pity instead of being transparent. (For the record, I am one of the people who appreciates when someone is real. I find comfort knowing others' struggles. If it seems easy to someone, I wonder what I'm doing wrong.) But I've also learned the importance of finding *your* people, the ones who can carry your story and help you work it out.

Work it out means exactly what it implies. It means doing the work to figure out what you're feeling and why. It means digging into the emotions you don't like to disturb and getting to the bottom of the hurt.

Sometimes it takes tough conversations to figure out if what you heard was what was meant. Bad communication and missed opportunities to encourage someone can lead the tenderhearted to conclusions that weren't intended. A simple conversation asking, "Hey, did you mean this?" can erase the tension and keep you from getting stuck in a whirlwind of hurt. Clarity is key. Maybe you took it exactly how they intended. That conversation might be enough for them to apologize or at least to get to the bottom of it.

Be transparent with those you can trust; work through the emotions to get to the roots; and finally, and most important, let God have the last word. That means letting your Christian friends hold you accountable.

Find friends who will hold you to the truth and keep you on solid biblical ground. That might mean correcting you if you are thinking the worst about someone who hurt you or reminding you that the person who died wasn't always right and your life before wasn't perfect either. There were trials then. There are trials now. God was with you before. He's with you now.

And finally, to reconcile the past, you need to know this. I've read the Bible my whole adult life. I've heard this section of Scripture many, many times, and yet I didn't live like it was my identity until recently. When you and I are in Christ, we aren't victims; we're conquerors. Let that sink in for a minute.

Romans chapter 8 begins, **"Therefore, there is now no condemnation for those who are in Christ Jesus"** (verse 1). *Condemnation* means strong disapproval. When you are a child of God, you aren't a failure, problem, or a mistake. You aren't worthless or too much or overwhelming. Not to God. God doesn't think less of you because of what you've been through, and he doesn't condemn you if you were the instigator. You aren't disqualified if you fell off the bandwagon, made the wrong choice that night, swiped when you should have turned it off. Forgiven in Christ means paid in full.

The apostle Paul goes on to explain that we no longer need to live in our flesh (as defeated), but we can live (victorious) in the Spirit. And then he says:

> **What, then, shall we say in response to these things? If God is for us, who can be against us? He who did not spare his own Son, but gave him up for us all—how will he not also, along with him, graciously give us all things? Who will bring any charge against those whom God has chosen? It is God who justifies. Who then is the one who condemns? No one. Christ Jesus who died—more than that, who was raised to life—is at the right hand of God and is also interceding for us. Who shall separate us from the love of Christ? Shall trouble or hardship or persecution or famine or nakedness or danger or sword? . . .**

> **No, in all these things we are more than conquerors through him who loved us. For I am convinced that neither death nor life, neither angels nor demons, neither the present nor the future, nor any powers, neither height nor depth, nor anything else in all creation, will be able to separate us from the love of God that is in Christ Jesus our Lord.** (Romans 8:31-35,37-39)

Is God for you? Yes! You are a child of God. He is your heavenly Father. That means it doesn't matter who says what about you. You have an audience of one, and he is crazy about you. How do you know? He gave his beloved Son to be brutally beaten and killed so you can be with him forever. Nothing you did can separate you from God, and nothing you've been through makes him think less of you.

He willingly gives you all things. Everything you need. Do you need grace because you messed up again? He's got it. Do you need confidence to believe you are worthy? You are his child, chosen and precious to him. Do you need strength to get through the storm you are in? His strength never runs out. Do you need a new job, help with a relationship, wisdom to know what to do and how to do it? His resources are limitless.

Christ is interceding for you. Have you considered the importance of that statement? Jesus became human. He knows what it is to be tired, lonely, and scared. He understands how much it hurts to be humiliated and cast aside and rejected. And he knows what you need, when you need it, and the best way to get it to you. Jesus is on your side.

If all this is in your favor, who dares to set themselves against you, and if they do, who cares? God is on your side. Jesus is interceding. Who cares that your ex-husband or that person on social media or that group of people talk about you and make fun of you and treat you cruelly? Even if Satan himself comes against you, nothing can touch you that doesn't first pass through the hands of a God who loves you.

Jesus is on your side.

Can they hurt you? Yes. But nothing—not angels, demons, time, space, even life itself—can cause God to love you less or take away what he has prepared for you. The minute you take your last breath here you will be with God in heaven forever. And that's why you can walk around like you won it all. You are a conqueror—not a bully demanding your way—but a person who belongs, no matter what your past looks like.

You and I *can* reconcile the past. We can move forward even as we work through the pain. As conquerors, we can move forward bravely, doing the important work God has for us to do in his kingdom.

The apostle Paul said, **"Brothers and sisters, . . . one thing I do: Forgetting what is behind and straining toward what is ahead, I press on toward the goal to win the prize for which God has called me heavenward in Christ Jesus"** (Philippians 3:13,14).

Do you know Paul's past? He tried to destroy the church

of God. But when God brought him out of the darkness of unbelief and into the light, Paul did not let his past paralyze him.

Nothing stopped the apostle Paul. When he could, he traveled to new places to tell people about Jesus. Being beaten, shipwrecked, and thrown out of town didn't deter him. If he wasn't accepted in one place, he went to the next. When he was imprisoned, he wrote letters. When he was chained to guards, he told them about Jesus. And above all, he prayed.

If one door closed, he waited for the next to open. If he despaired of life, it taught him to rely on God. If he needed someone to comfort him, he rejoiced that he learned how to comfort others.

Nothing is wasted. Not in my life. Not in yours. Whatever you did or endured, it all became a part of the story of God's redemption in your life. He will use it to help you minister to others.

And you've got a lot of ministry to do. So work it out and get moving, confident that with Christ you can.

WHAT DOES THIS MEAN FOR YOU?

1. If you're going to start the process of healing, you have to confront the past hurt. It took me eight years to realize that confronting a problem and becoming a target shook my identity. What have you believed about yourself because of the hurt you've experienced or caused in the past?

2. In John 8:44, Jesus says that the devil **"was a murderer from the beginning, not holding to the truth, for there is no truth in him. When he lies, he speaks his native language, for he is a liar and the father of lies."** The only way to combat the lies of Satan is to know the truth God gives in Scripture. Below are some common lies and some passages for you to look up if these are the lies you've believed.

    a. I'm not worthy of love: Psalm 86; Titus 3:4–7; Jeremiah 31:3,4; Ephesians 2:4–10; Zephaniah 3:17
    b. God can't use me: Exodus 4:10–12; Isaiah 6:1–8; Jeremiah 1:4–7; 1 Corinthians 1:26–29
    c. I don't matter: Matthew 6:25,26; Matthew 10:29–31; Psalm 56:8
    d. God can't forgive this: Psalm 103; 1 Timothy 1:15–17
    e. God doesn't care about me because he let this happen: Romans 8:28–39; Isaiah 63:9
    f. I'm not strong enough to get through this: Romans 8:37; 2 Corinthians 12:9–11; Judges 6:11–16

3. Jesus said, **"Love your enemies and pray for those who persecute you"** (Matthew 5:44). I am convinced that praying for the people who hurt you is the key to healing. Pray they come to a closer walk with God, repent and turn from their sin if they haven't, and become useful people

in God's kingdom. Pray God forgives them the same way he has forgiven you. As you pray this over and over, your heart changes. Bitterness disappears. Resentment dissolves. And the pain becomes manageable. If you hurt others with your words or actions, pray that God heals the people you hurt and that they come to fully know God's love. Pray that God restores them in ways that you can't. And pray God helps you to know the freedom of forgiveness without shame. Write out a prayer for the people who have hurt you or whom you have hurt. Every time you hurt or feel shame, come back to this page and pray it again.

CHAPTER 2

Confident That Prayer Moves the Hand of God

I grew up with a praying grandpa. When he prayed, things happened. In fact, I attribute the fact that I work in God's kingdom at least in part thanks to his prayers, even though he didn't live to see them answered. When I was 19, I moved in with him and my grandma to attend the university a few miles from their house. Despite the fact that I grew up Christian, had read through my Bible, and in theory was ready to serve the Lord, I was also restless and adamantly strong-willed. I had big plans to write secular fiction and was completely engrossed in a liberal arts education to make that happen.

Grandpa had a debilitating stroke a few years before I moved in, so he wasn't able to argue with me. I'm certain he prayed that God would use whatever talents and abilities I had for God's kingdom and not for my own glory.

After my grandpa died, my mother took over the role of prayer warrior. No matter the situation, Mom prayed. Once during the first year of my marriage, my mom drove in to our driveway, heard my husband and me arguing through our open windows, drove back to the end of the driveway, prayed, and drove away. She didn't tell me about the incident for several years. She determined that we needed prayer more than anything else that day.

Prayer is communicating with God.

Prayer is communicating with God. It is the act of involving God in your life, asking for his direction (wisdom and discernment), and praying that his will is done through and around you.

There is no prescribed way to do this. You can speak out loud or in your head. You can kneel, sit, lie down, stand. You can pray for hours or for a few seconds.

In the Bible, Moses talked to God face-to-face. David inquired of the Lord. Daniel got down on his knees three times a day to pray.

You can address God as God, Father, Lord, Jesus, Holy Spirit, or several versions and variations of those names: heavenly Father, Jesus, the Lamb of God, holy Lord, Creator, Maker, Counselor, Friend.

There are only a few imperatives when it comes to prayer. The writer of Hebrews tells us this: **"And without faith it is impossible to please God, because anyone who comes to him must believe that he exists and that he rewards those who earnestly seek him"** (11:6). And James adds: **"If any of you lacks wisdom, you should ask God, who gives generously to all without finding fault, and it will be given**

to you. But when you ask, you must believe and not doubt, because the one who doubts is like a wave of the sea, blown and tossed by the wind. That person should not expect to receive anything from the Lord" (1:5–7).

So then, prayer is not a matter of praying to a god if a god exists. It is not wishful thinking or positive energy sent throughout the universe. God exists whether you believe he exists or not. When you pray, you must believe he exists and that he answers prayer. If you don't believe he exists and you doubt he'll answer your prayers, your prayers will not be answered.

What should you pray about? The Bible gives quite a few examples and ideas.

In Genesis chapter 18, Abraham pleaded with God to spare Sodom and Gomorrah. What an example for us to pray for God to spare cities and countries while opening up opportunities for the Word of God to spread.

In 1 Samuel chapter 1, a woman named Hannah prayed that God would give her a son and if he did, she promised to give him back to God for service in his kingdom. Her prayer is a beautiful reminder for us to pray specifically for God to equip our children and others to work in his kingdom.

The Psalms are prayers of David and others. Some ask God for deliverance from an enemy or sin, some praise God, and some ask God why or how long will they need to wait or where he is. All these are sentiments that are easy for you and me to relate to.

In the Old Testament, when an enemy army, the

Assyrians, and their leader, Sennacherib, came to destroy Judah, King Hezekiah prayed:

> **"Lord, the God of Israel, enthroned between the cherubim, you alone are God over all the kingdoms of the earth. You have made heaven and earth. Give ear, Lord, and hear; open your eyes, Lord, and see; listen to the words Sennacherib has sent to ridicule the living God.**
>
> **"It is true, Lord, that the Assyrian kings have laid waste these nations and their lands. They have thrown their gods into the fire and destroyed them, for they were not gods but only wood and stone, fashioned by human hands. Now, Lord our God, deliver us from his hand, so that all the kingdoms of the earth may know that you alone, Lord, are God."** (2 Kings 19:15–19)

Hezekiah and the people of Judah were in grave danger and prayed God would rescue them from this advancing army. How important for you and me to pray that God would foil any evil set against us. Pray that God's name and his people would be a light, shining God's glory for all to see. Pray that evil men would be stopped and that God would protect our borders and secure our land. And ask God to help us identify and rid our lives of any source of security other than him.

Later, Hezekiah became ill. Isaiah the prophet came to him and told Hezekiah he would die. **"Hezekiah turned his face to the wall and prayed to the Lord, 'Remember, Lord, how I have walked before you faithfully and with wholehearted devotion and have done what is good in your eyes.' And Hezekiah wept bitterly"** (2 Kings 20:2,3). God, in return, added 15 years to Hezekiah's life. We too can pray for the sick and dying. Who knows if God will relent and add years to those who are faithfully serving him or give additional time to those who don't yet know him. If God is preparing to bring a loved one home, we pray for God's peace to be with them and that God would bring them to a swift and peaceful earthly end.

In the book of Esther, the Jews fasted for three days, and commentaries note that prayer was certainly included in the fast. The Jews sought God to deliver them from the king's decree that would destroy them (Esther 4:16). Often, we face impending peril, not only physically but spiritually or emotionally. We too need to take this to heart and gather with friends and bring the situation before the throne of God.

In Daniel chapter 2, some young men named Daniel, Shadrach, Meshach, and Abednego prayed God would reveal King Nebuchadnezzar's dream to them to spare them from being put to death (Daniel 2:18). Everyday believers in other parts of the world are endangered. We can pray that God makes them invisible to those who would harm them and that he opens secret paths for them to continue to carry the gospel message. We can pray for all those in harm's way. We can pray for anyone caught in slavery to be released and for the death of innocent lives to stop.

Jesus taught his disciples and us to pray the Lord's Prayer. In it, Jesus told us to pray that we represent God well, that we act in accordance with God's good and gracious will which is carried out perfectly in heaven. He told us to pray for our basic necessities and for forgiveness. We also pray for forgiving hearts to forgive the people who have wronged us. And finally, Jesus' prayer included petitions for help in overcoming temptation and rescue from everything the devil and his army would throw our way (Matthew 6:9-13; Luke 11:2-4).

Jesus prayed that his followers would be in the world but not of the world (John 17) and that we would be set apart by the truth. It's important for you and me to pray for this too! The world is evil, and evil seeps into our souls. You can pray to be set apart and for God to help you not to be tainted or jaded by all you see and hear. You can pray for self-control to set limits to what you let in.

Jesus also prayed that if there was another way to rescue the world from sin without him having to experience the gruesome death ahead of him, that God would provide another way (Matthew 26:42). You too can pray for easier roads when life is hard. *"God, help! Open a door! Foil the plans of any evil force that is at work that is trying to keep me from doing the important work I have to do."*

In the book of Acts, the disciples prayed for clarity in choosing a replacement for Judas (Acts 1:24,25), for boldness to speak God's Word, and for it to be backed up with signs and wonders (Acts 4:30). You can pray for clarity often. You often don't know what is best, and you can't see into hearts. Who doesn't need to pray for boldness to proclaim God's Word mightily and often?

You can pray for clarity.

The Christian martyr Stephen prayed for God to receive his spirit as he died and for the people stoning him to be forgiven (Acts 7:59,60). If you are conscious before death, you too can pray for God to receive your spirit and for anyone who has wronged you to be forgiven and to seek God's grace.

Saul, who became the apostle Paul after being converted, was blind and praying after Jesus appeared to him on the road to Damascus (Acts 9:11). We aren't told what he was praying, but we know the Lord heard him because God sent Ananias to Paul to restore his sight. Peter prayed beside the bed of a dead woman and then raised her back to life (Acts 9:40). The church in Jerusalem prayed for the deliverance of Peter when he was imprisoned by Herod, who had already put James to death (Acts 12:1–5). The church in Antioch prayed a blessing over Paul and Barnabas before they left on a mission trip (Acts 13:3). You pray wonderful things when you pray for freedom for captives, blessings for the work of those proclaiming the gospel, and for God to hear and answer the prayers of all the saints who come before him in prayer.

The apostle Paul prayed so many prayers. If you have time and the desire to study them, type this into your browser: "All the prayers of Paul." You can see them listed and/or print them off to study them further. But here are some of the things the apostle Paul prayed:

- He thanked God for the believers (a lot!) (Romans 1:8–10; Philippians 1:3–6; Colossians 1:3; 1 Thessalonians 1:2,3; 2 Thessalonians 1:3–5; Philemon 1:4–7)
- He prayed for people to be saved. (Romans 10:1)
- He prayed people would live in harmony with one another. (Romans 15:5,6)
- He prayed God would fill believers with joy and peace so they would abound in hope. (Romans 15:13)
- He prayed to be delivered from unbelievers so that he could continue ministry. (Romans 15:30–32; 2 Thessalonians 3:2–5)
- He prayed believers wouldn't do wrong, would be sanctified (set apart), and would be kept blameless. (2 Corinthians 13:7–9; 1 Thessalonians 5:23,24)
- He prayed that God would give believers the Spirit of wisdom and revelation to know God and the greatness of his power. (Ephesians 1:15–23)
- He prayed Christ would dwell in hearts so they would comprehend the love of Christ. (Ephesians 3:14–21)
- He prayed to proclaim the gospel boldly. (Ephesians 6:19,20)

- He prayed believers would know the peace of God that surpasses understanding. (Philippians 4:6,7; 2 Thessalonians 3:16)
- He prayed believers would be filled with the knowledge of God's will to walk in a manner worthy of God and to be strengthened in power for great endurance. (Colossians 1:9–11)
- He prayed for God to open doors for the Word. (Colossians 4:2–4)

All these are important and good prayers to pray! In addition, Paul advised believers to pray for all those in authority so that we might lead peaceful and quiet lives (1 Timothy 2:1–3). And perhaps most poignantly, Paul reminded us that prayer is sometimes hard. He said:

> **In the same way, the Spirit helps us in our weakness. We do not know what we ought to pray for, but the Spirit himself intercedes for us through wordless groans. And he who searches our hearts knows the mind of the Spirit, because the Spirit intercedes for God's people in accordance with the will of God.** (Romans 8:26,27)

When you don't know how to pray and the mess seems too big to comprehend, when you don't know how to untangle all the pieces or who is right or what is true, you can pray confidently because God knows and understands. You don't even need to know what to pray. You can simply go to God and say, *"HELP! Untangle what I can't. Work in ways I can't comprehend. Do more than I know to ask you to do."*

God knows and understands.

All this is fine and good, but can you be sure God hears your prayers? And how do you know your prayers make a difference?

There are many passages, so here are just a few. Psalm 145:18 says, **"The Lord is near to all who call on him, to all who call on him in truth."**

How do you call to God in truth? The note in my study Bible says that "in truth" refers to "godly integrity."[2] Interestingly, the definition of *integrity* is "to live honestly." It is possible to lie in your prayers, but you shouldn't expect God to answer them if you do. Sometimes you and I let our anger color a situation. We may think we are right and the other person is wrong, but God may see something very different. God not only sees what happened; he knows the motives behind the actions. **"All a person's ways seem pure to them, but motives are weighed by the Lord"** (Proverbs 16:2). So when you pray, if the situation is emotional, you would be wise to go humbly before God and admit your anger or your hurt and ask for clarity even if it means God shows you that you are wrong!

Psalm 34:15–18 says,

> **The eyes of the Lord are on the righteous, and his ears are attentive to their cry; but the face of the**

Lord is against those who do evil, to blot out their name from the earth.

The righteous cry out, and the Lord hears them; he delivers them from all their troubles. The Lord is close to the brokenhearted and saves those who are crushed in spirit.

James 5:16 echoes the same sentiment: **"The prayer of a righteous person is powerful and effective."**

The reasonable question after looking at both of these passages is to ask, *"Who is righteous, and how do I become righteous so my prayers are powerful, effective, and heard by God?"*

There's only one way to become righteous, or to have right standing, with God. The apostle Paul put it this way: **"God made him who had no sin to be sin for us, so that in him we might become the righteousness of God"** (2 Corinthians 5:21).

Jesus lived a perfect life for us and took all the sins that have ever been committed and ever will be committed on himself while hanging on a cross. He paid the debt you and I never could. Now, we are declared innocent, not because of what we've done but because of what Christ did.

We tend to focus on the second half of James 5:16. But the first half of the verse is equally important. It says, **"Therefore confess your sins to each other and pray for each other so that you may be healed."**

To *confess* is "to admit your faults." Maybe you aren't

so great at doing this. Years ago, people used to go to confession before taking Lord's Supper. The pastor would hear their sins and proclaim the repentant heart forgiven. Then the person would take Lord's Supper, knowing Christ's death made them right before God.

You *might* confess your sins to God, but you would rather no one else knows the things you do wrong and certainly not the things you struggle with still. But James says that is the opposite approach to the one you should take. It is in the confessing and the subsequent prayers of your fellow Christians that you are healed.

Satan loves silence. As long as you keep your sin to yourself, he can convince you that no one else struggles, that God hates you or wouldn't forgive *that* sin. You don't have the benefit and blessing of praying for each other if no one knows!

Satan loves silence.

And here's why you may want to rethink this. Isaiah 59:1,2 says, **"Surely the arm of the Lord is not too short to save, nor his ear too dull to hear. But your iniquities have separated you from your God; your sins have hidden his face from you, so that he will not hear."**

Your sins are a barrier between you and God, and that isn't God's desire for your life. He wants you to be free. Jesus said, **"If the Son sets you free, you will be free indeed"** (John 8:36). Free, as in not in bondage to anything. Free from the addiction that is eating you up and free from the consequences of the sin you keep falling into.

Don't misunderstand. I'm not saying you won't struggle anymore. In fact, I just gave a friend two sheets of temporary tattoos to use in his counseling ministry. The message: "If you struggle with sin, you're in." As long as you're on earth, you will be saying with the apostle Paul:

> **For I do not do the good I want to do, but the evil I do not want to do—this I keep on doing. Now if I do what I do not want to do, it is no longer I who do it, but it is sin living in me that does it.**
>
> **So I find this law at work: Although I want to do good, evil is right there with me. For in my inner being I delight in God's law; but I see another law at work in me, waging war against the law of my mind and making me a prisoner of the law of sin at work within me. What a wretched man I am! Who will rescue me from this body that is subject to death? Thanks be to God, who delivers me through Jesus Christ our Lord!"** (Romans 7:19–25)

Are you confused?

You'll never be perfect, but the key is to find the people you trust to help you through when you are struggling with temptation. Open up to them; be vulnerable; let people in who will pray for you, hold you accountable, and encourage you.

James gives another reason why you might not be getting what you ask: **"When you ask, you do not receive,**

because you ask with wrong motives, that you may spend what you get on your pleasures" (4:3). Already in the first chapters of Genesis, God noted this about the human heart: **"The Lord saw how great the wickedness of the human race had become on the earth, and that every inclination of the thoughts of the human heart was only evil all the time"** (Genesis 6:5).

You and I think about ourselves far more than we should. Even when we want to think about others, we have a tendency to think about how something affects us, if it's good for us, and what about what we want?

God looks at the needs and desires of everyone when he answers prayers, and he always answers in the way that is best for everyone. A great way to see more of your prayers become reality is to take Psalm 37:4 to heart: **"Take delight in the Lord, and he will give you the desires of your heart."**

When you take delight in the things that God delights in, your prayers will align with God's heart. You do this as you pray all these things the Bible shows you to pray about.

A lot of times you don't know what God has in store. You pray not knowing if it's God's will to heal you or to give you the strength to carry on. That's why when you pray, you let God be God. He may give you what you ask immediately. He may give you what you ask eventually. And sometimes he says no. The apostle Paul reports:

> **Therefore, in order to keep me from becoming conceited, I was given a thorn in my flesh, a**

> **messenger of Satan, to torment me. Three times I pleaded with the Lord to take it away from me. But he said to me, "My grace is sufficient for you, for my power is made perfect in weakness."** (2 Corinthians 12:7-9)

Here's what I know. Far too many of us err by not praying. We rely on google. We go to friends. We explore TikTok or Instagram for wisdom instead of God who created the universe, knows all the stars by name, and invites us to ask.

Here's something else I know. God loves us and wants what's best for us. The apostle John tells us, **"This is the confidence we have in approaching God: that if we ask anything according to his will, he hears us. And if we know that he hears us—whatever we ask—we know that we have what we asked of him"** (1 John 5:14,15).

I'm a parent. I absolutely love doing things for my children that I know will help them. My son and daughter-in-law just moved. I asked if I could prepare meals for the movers. My heart was overflowing when I had a full table of mostly guys eating meatballs and scalloped potatoes and cookies.

God is our Father. He loves us. Jesus said, **"If you, then, though you are evil, know how to give good gifts to your children, how much more will your Father in heaven give good gifts to those who ask him!"** (Matthew 7:11).

Why would you think he wouldn't want to hear your

heart's desires or wouldn't love to give you what would please him to give you? Why would he offer so many invitations throughout the Bible telling you to bring your needs to him if he was annoyed and irritated if you did? He wouldn't.

So be a person of prayer. Be the one praying for those who are straying from the faith, for this country, for your church, for your children, for your marriage. Don't assume someone else will do it.

Ezekiel 22:30 is one of the saddest verses in the Bible: **"I looked for someone among them who would build up the wall and stand before me in the gap on behalf of the land so I would not have to destroy it, but I found no one."**

No one called out on behalf of the land. No one asked God to intervene. No one took steps or measures to bring people back to God. No one.

God was looking.

He's still watching. Will you stand in the gap? Will you take the time to pray confidently?

WHAT DOES THIS MEAN FOR YOU?

1. What keeps you from praying for the things that are on your heart?

2. Make a list of the biggest complaints in your life right now. Be specific.

3. This is now your prayer list. Put these names and situations on a note card. Keep it by your bed or wherever you

will be able to see it. Pray for those people and situations often throughout the day.

4. Read Acts 12:1–19. Note the seriousness of the situation (verses 1–4). The church had one recourse. Note verses 5 and 12. How was the church praying?

5. Are you earnest enough about the things in your life to gather with other Christians and pray? Who are two or three other people you will gather to pray with you?

CHAPTER 3

Confident That God Isn't Bothered When You Ask for Little Things

I don't know why we don't take small things to God in prayer. Is it because we don't think it's worth his time or because we think we should be able to handle things on our own? All too often, even the seemingly little things are beyond our ability to fix. These small, everyday things can remind us how much we need God every day.

There is an interesting verse in the Bible that teaches a big lesson. It's found in 2 Chronicles 16:12: **"In the thirty-ninth year of his reign Asa was afflicted with a disease in his feet. Though his disease was severe, even in his illness he did not seek help from the Lord, but only from the physicians."**

The chapter just before this covers King Asa's reforms. Asa served the Lord wholeheartedly and helped the people remove their idols and return to the Lord. People from other territories came back to Asa's territory in large numbers when they saw the Lord was with Asa (15:9).

As time went on, Asa started to rely on people rather than God. He aligned himself with the king of Aram rather than asking God for help. God sent a prophet named Hanani to rebuke Asa. Hanani said:

> **"Because you relied on the king of Aram and not on the Lord your God, the army of the king of Aram has escaped from your hand. Were not the Cushites and Libyans a mighty army with great numbers of chariots and horsemen? Yet when you relied on the Lord, he delivered them into your hand. For the eyes of the Lord range throughout the earth to strengthen those whose hearts are fully committed to him. You have done a foolish thing, and from now on you will be at war."** (2 Chronicles 16:7–9)

Instead of repenting, Asa put the prophet in prison. The next verse says, **"At the same time Asa brutally oppressed some of the people"** (16:10).

In his commentary on 2 Chronicles, Paul Wendland sheds further light on what was happening:

> It is a great pity that Asa did not respond to the prophet's plain-speaking ways with a forthright confession, as David his father had. Instead, we see him react in a way common to those who don't

> like the message God sends them. They become angry with the messenger. So angry did Asa become, in fact, that he put Hanani in prison. The Hebrew word for prison connotes some sort of physical torture—"a twisted place," literally. Perhaps this refers to the practice of holding prisoners in uncomfortable positions—limbs distorted—in devices like stocks. Jeremiah, we know, suffered a similar fate (Jeremiah 20:2). Asa, the first king to begin a reformation at the encouragement of a prophet, also becomes the first king mentioned in Scripture to physically abuse a prophet.
>
> His anger was not satisfied with the torture of a man of God. He also "brutally oppressed" some of his own people, very likely those who had sided with the prophet.[3]

In light of this, the note in my study Bible on 2 Chronicles 16:12 concerning Asa's disease in his feet makes more sense. It reads: "For other examples of disease as punishment for sin see 2 Chronicles 21:16–20; 26:16–23; Acts 12:23. Cf. 2 Kings 15:5."[4]

God allowed this king who had done great and amazing things to suffer, and in his suffering, God hoped Asa would turn to him so he could heal him and show him his favor again. But Asa didn't turn to him for healing, and healing didn't come.

Wendland points out that the issue was not in seeking a doctor's help but rather in relying only on the doctors while refusing to seek the Lord.

Maybe in your mind a foot disease is *not* a small thing. Maybe you would've prayed about it. What about an ingrown toenail or a baby who won't sleep or a myriad of otherwise seemingly mundane things? Do you pray about those?

My fourth child's birth was traumatic, which caused her to have severe bruising. Because of it she had more red blood cells to break down, which caused too much bilirubin, jaundice, and a sleepy baby who wouldn't eat and had to be placed under a special light to break the bilirubin down. Having a baby who didn't want to eat delayed my breast milk from coming in, so I had a baby who was ready to eat, and I had nothing to give her.

I distinctly remember my prayer: *"God, you tell us to ask for daily bread. My daughter needs milk, and I can't make it come in. But you can, and I'm trusting you and asking you to provide what she needs."*

A few hours later, my milk came in. Breast milk may seem like a silly thing to pray about.

What's worthy of your prayers and what isn't?

Even as I write that, I hear my mother quoting James: **"You do not have because you do not ask God"** (James 4:2). God can say no if it is not in your best interest. By why would you fail to ask him?

I travel a lot. Often when I get in my car, I ask God to go before me, behind me, and to be beside me. I sometimes, but not always, pray, "Lord, keep the animals off the road." On my last trip home from Appleton, Wisconsin, I saw deer standing next to the road on three separate occasions. It was as if they were standing still, waiting, almost as if they had been commanded not to cross yet.

Isaiah 31:1–3 records God's words to his people:

> **Woe to those who go down to Egypt for help, who rely on horses, who trust in the multitude of their chariots and in the great strength of their horsemen, but do not look to the Holy One of Israel, or seek help from the LORD. Yet he too is wise and can bring disaster; he does not take back his words. He will rise up against that wicked nation, against those who help evildoers. But the Egyptians are mere mortals and not God; their horses are flesh and not spirit.**

How often our prayers show this mentality! We love to rely on men and their wisdom and what they think is best. I was recently in a text thread with two friends. One has been having health problems. She sent a list of prayer requests including one that she gets in to see the right doctor and that the doctor orders the right tests.

My first response is always to pray for total healing. But God may choose to heal her through the work of doctors and the medicines they prescribe. There is nothing wrong with asking for help in the little things.

God isn't bothered by your requests of little things, even if the request is for something as seemingly insignificant as having meat to eat. The Israelites had left Egypt and were traveling through the desert. God was raining bread down from heaven to feed the people, but some troublemakers (my Bible says "rabble," a word that I love!) started complaining that they didn't have meat. In Egypt they had meat and all kinds of vegetables and spices, but in the desert, it was manna every day. So Moses complained to the Lord.

God isn't bothered by your requests of little things.

The problem was not that the people craved meat. The problem was that the people didn't go to God in prayer and pray for meat. Instead, this group of troublemakers spread discontent throughout the camp.

Moses' complaint is one of the more entertaining parts of the Bible, not because it is right but because it is honest. Moses said:

> **"Did I conceive all these people? Did I give them birth? Why do you tell me to carry them in my arms, as a nurse carries an infant, to the land you promised on oath to their ancestors? Where can I get meat for all these people? They keep wailing to me, 'Give us meat to eat!' I cannot carry all these people by myself; the burden is too heavy for me. If this is how you are going to treat me, please go**

> **ahead and kill me—if I have found favor in your eyes—and do not let me face my own ruin."** (Numbers 11:12–15)

Moses had a meltdown. "Look, God, the people want meat. And, honestly, it's just too much. In fact, you know what? Just kill me."

God's response was first of all to get 70 men together to help Moses lead. Not 1 or 2 helpers but 70! Then God said, **"You will not eat** [meat] **for just one day, or two days, or five, ten or twenty days, but for a whole month—until it comes out of your nostrils and you loathe it—because you have rejected the LORD, who is among you, and have wailed before him, saying, 'Why did we ever leave Egypt?'"** (Numbers 11:19,20).

Moses didn't get it. Looking around, he couldn't see feeding two million people meat as a realistic possibility.

> **"Here I am among six hundred thousand men on foot, and you say, 'I will give them meat to eat for a whole month!' Would they have enough if flocks and herds were slaughtered for them? Would they have enough if all the fish in the sea were caught for them?"**
>
> **The LORD answered Moses, "Is the LORD's arm too short? Now you will see whether or not what I say will come true for you."** (11:21–23).

"Is the Lord's arm too short?" is not a familiar phrase to you and me. Three other times in the Bible similar wording about God's arm is used. Deuteronomy 26:8 says, **"So the Lord brought us out of Egypt with a mighty hand and an outstretched arm, with great terror and with signs and wonders."** Isaiah 52:10 says, **"The Lord will lay bare his holy arm in the sight of all the nations, and all the ends of the earth will see the salvation of our God."** And finally, Isaiah 59:1 says, **"Surely the arm of the Lord is not too short to save, nor his ear too dull to hear."**

The note in my study Bible for Isaiah 59:1 directs me back to the note on Isaiah 51:5, which notes that the arm symbolizes power (think of a muscular guy flexing, only better because it's God). Several blog posts I read offered another explanation. Our arms don't reach very far. We can maybe grasp something two or three feet away. God asking Moses if his arm is too short is akin to asking: "Is this outside my reach? Is this too much for me to handle? Step aside Moses. Watch and be amazed."

Meat is not a big deal, except when it's for two million or so people wandering in a desert. God's point in all this was that it was easy enough to do. All they had to do was ask instead of complaining and inferring they were better off as slaves to heathens in Egypt than they were under God's care in the desert.

So go ahead and confidently ask God to help with your menopause symptoms or your cranky neighbor or for your child to get into their first-choice college (and get a scholarship!) or for your baby to take a little longer nap. I was so tired with one of my newborns that I asked God for four straight hours of sleep one day, and that's exactly what I got. When I told my brother, he said, "Amber, you should have asked for six!" Maybe I should have, but I was thrilled with four.

God is not offended by your prayers for seemingly small things. He's offended when you don't go to him at all or when you seek answers from everyone but him. Be confident in your small prayers to a big God!

WHAT DOES THIS MEAN FOR YOU?

1. I just asked my teen and young adult children what small prayers they have prayed recently. One prayed to get her hoop earring shut. One prayed for a parking spot in Glacier National Park. They prayed to get to places on time and not to run out of gas. What does it show God when you pray about little things?

2. Read 2 Kings 6:1–7. Why was it such a big deal that the ax-head fell into the water?

   The prophet knew to go to Elisha. Elisha, through the power of God, was able to make the ax-head float. You may not be able to make things float miraculously, but you can certainly ask God to help you retrieve what needs to be retrieved. Whether it is your car keys or your wedding ring, God knows EXACTLY where they are when you don't! What are the small things in your life you need to start praying about?

CHAPTER 4

Confident You Aren't Asking Too Much

All too often when things fall apart, we fall apart too. God isn't our first resort or even on the radar because we are too busy freaking out. If there's one thing we need to get into our heads, one habit we need to work on becoming routine, it is going to God knowing he is our hope. There is hope, no matter how bad things look.

One year ago, things were as bad as they could be between me and one of my children. This child was making choices that were devastating to my husband and me. In fact, almost exactly a year ago, I was speaking to a moms group at Pastor Mike Novotny's church in Appleton, Wisconsin. I had spent the night at the home of a woman who opens her home regularly to me. As I was getting ready that morning, another of my children called to tell me what the other child was doing in my absence. My heart broke. But I had a whole day of ministry ahead of me.

I spoke to the moms group and did an interview with

Pastor Mike. In between those things, I had a chance to hang out with one of the camera operators for the interview. Because he's a nice guy and a good listener, I told him the situation. He assured me he would pray. Another friend met me after lunch, and we walked loops inside the church for almost an hour. She comforted me with details of her own child's rebellion and the life this child had years later, following God.

Shortly after that day, a couple from my church stopped by my house. Their child was not making good decisions either. Right then we started praying. A few weeks later, we called more friends and asked them to gather, and we prayed for their child and my child and the other children who needed guidance and help just as much as ours.

You can't imagine all that changed in just a few months. Drastic, almost unbelievable changes occurred in our children's lives.

No matter what the situation and how dire it is, you can be confident it isn't too much for God. In fact, it is in the impossible that you realize just how much you need God. Your resources are terribly inadequate to fix anything; God is your only hope.

The gospel writer Mark talks about an incident that occurred on the Sea of Galilee. It is of the we-have-suddenly-happened-upon-disaster variety. Mark's account shows that even when things are completely out of control, it takes so very little for God to set them right.

> **That day when evening came,** [Jesus] **said to his disciples, "Let us go over to the other side." Leaving the crowd behind, they took him along, just as he was, in the boat. There were also other boats with him. A furious squall came up, and the waves broke over the boat, so that it was nearly swamped. Jesus was in the stern, sleeping on a cushion. The disciples woke him and said to him, "Teacher, don't you care if we drown?"**
>
> **He got up, rebuked the wind and said to the waves, "Quiet! Be still!" Then the wind died down and it was completely calm.**
>
> **He said to his disciples, "Why are you so afraid? Do you still have no faith?"**
>
> **They were terrified and asked each other, "Who is this? Even the wind and the waves obey him!"** (4:35–41)

This account becomes a little more incredible when you remember that at least four of these disciples had formerly been experienced professional fishermen, and squalls were not uncommon on the Sea of Galilee. This storm was different. It was furious, violent, intense. The disciples were not being dramatic. They had done what they could do, and they thought they were about to die.

Three words stilled the storm. Three. And that shook the disciples as much as being in the storm. To go from thinking they were going to die to total calm in a matter of seconds requires a little recalibration. But not for Jesus, because he understood he would not die before his time; he, even in human form with his power restrained, was in total control.

Three words stilled the storm.

Do you understand what that means for your life? Psalm 139:16 says, **"Your eyes saw my unformed body; all the days ordained for me were written in your book before one of them came to be."**

Long before you took your first breath, God had already determined when you would take your last. You will never be in a situation that is beyond the scope and realm of God's power. No car or train or plane crash. No disease. No trauma. No storm.

Do your prayers even matter then? Do you have to worry about putting your life in danger and shortening what otherwise may have been a long life? Can you binge on the wrong foods and beverages and live a sedentary lifestyle and take years off your life? Yes, yes, and yes. And God knew that you and I would do these things sometimes and took all these things into consideration when he wrote the number of our days in his book.

That storm on the Sea of Galilee lasted only a brief time. It was overwhelming but short-lived. It was a disaster averted. It was like a car careening toward you on a winter road that misses you by a few inches. Or a four-hour flight through a thunderstorm while you hang on for dear life but arrive shaken but whole. It's that incident when a child fell into the deep end of the pool but was rescued by someone who noticed and jumped in.

If your brain works like mine, then you have to pause. You know the opposite scenarios: the car accident that wasn't averted and lives were lost; the flights that went down instead of arriving safely at their destinations; the child who fell in the pool, but no one was there to notice and the body was pulled out later.

If only this wasn't a sinful world where these things happen! Jesus healed a lot of people, but he didn't heal everyone. The Bible tells of the people he raised from the dead: a synagogue leader's daughter, a widow's son, and a man named Lazarus. But there were a lot of people who didn't get raised.

Why her and not him? Why him and not her? Why did *this* tragedy come to your family and *that* tragedy go to theirs? Only God knows.

I've heard it said that if everyone put their struggles in a pile for all to see, most people would keep their own pile. God determines what he allows into our lives and for how long. One person goes through something for three months. Another goes through the same thing for a year. Another struggles for decades. Only God knows why.

Shortly after the account of the disciples in the storm, Mark records another impossible situation. This had been going on for considerably longer and caused a woman a great deal of pain:

> **And a woman was there who had been subject to bleeding for twelve years. She had suffered a great deal under the care of many doctors and had spent all she had, yet instead of getting better she grew worse. When she heard about Jesus, she came up behind him in the crowd and touched his cloak, because she thought, "If I just touch his clothes, I will be healed." Immediately her bleeding stopped and she felt in her body that she was freed from her suffering.**
>
> **At once Jesus realized that power had gone out from him. He turned around in the crowd and asked, "Who touched my clothes?"**
>
> **"You see the people crowding against you," his disciples answered, "and yet you can ask, 'Who touched me?'"**
>
> **But Jesus kept looking around to see who had done it. Then the woman, knowing what had happened to her, came and fell at his feet and, trembling with fear, told him the whole truth. He said to her, "Daughter, your faith has healed you. Go in peace and be freed from your suffering."** (Mark 5:25–34)

If you read that quickly, you may have missed how awful this woman's life was. Bleeding made her ceremonially unclean. It's hard to imagine just how much this would affect her. Leviticus 15:25–27 says:

> **"When a woman has a discharge of blood for many days at a time other than her monthly period or has a discharge that continues beyond her period, she will be unclean as long as she has the discharge, just as in the days of her period. Any bed she lies on while her discharge continues will be unclean, as is her bed during her monthly period, and anything she sits on will be unclean, as during her period. Anyone who touches them will be unclean; they must wash their clothes and bathe with water, and they will be unclean till evening."**

To be friends with her would mean having to wash rigorously and be considered unclean. She couldn't just hug someone or get a reassuring tap or go to a friend's house and sit down without making the house unclean. (I don't know what is going through your mind right now, but when I get to heaven, I'm going to find this woman and give her a long hug.) She would have been shunned by many, because to be near her or touch her would make them unclean, and that was too much work for most people.

In addition to the isolation, she "had suffered a great deal . . . and had spent all she had" on doctors, who not only failed to help her but made the suffering worse.

How this woman had the wherewithal to go to Jesus is beyond me. Sheer desperation must have driven her, because she was out of resources. Somehow she heard of Jesus, and despite the crowds, she went for it.

She didn't need to touch Jesus, but she believed she did. The note in my study Bible says, "Although it needed to be bolstered by physical contact, her faith was rewarded."[5] *Bolstered* means "to support, strengthen, to prop up." She had the faith to go to Jesus, but in her mind, the healing would take place when and if she touched his clothes: *"If I just touch his clothes, I will be healed."*

The woman who had a moment of courage suddenly trembled with fear when Jesus made her tell her story. You might ask why Jesus did this. First, so there would be no doubt how she had been healed. Many doctors had tried to cure her, and she had received many treatments. Jesus would get the glory from the healing, not them.

After so many years, many of those present probably knew who she was and treated her as an object of scorn because of her condition. They needed to hear she was healed.

And even more important than all these things, the word Jesus used for "healed" actually means "saved." When Jesus called her daughter (a term he used only that one time) and told her to "go in peace," he not only referred to her physical condition but her spiritual salvation.[6] The act of healing her convinced her that Jesus wasn't just a healer but the Son of God and her Savior. Jesus gave the woman even more than she knew to ask for and far more than she knew she needed. And it happened with just a touch of his cloak.

How many people were saved because of what they saw that day? When you and I struggle through hardships, it can be difficult to see any good that could come from the bad. But this woman's account is still reinforcing our faith today, two thousand years later.

If Jesus healed her, he can heal my marriage. If Jesus healed her, there's hope for your wandering son. If Jesus healed her when no one else could, then he certainly can fix the broken in our lives too.

Sometimes after a certain amount of time, some people quit praying. Four or nine or fifteen years have passed. If God was going to answer that prayer, wouldn't he have done so by now?

God works in his time frame, not ours. Before you quit praying, remember: Abraham waited for a son for 25 years. David was anointed king long before he took the throne. And he was king of little Hebron for seven years before he reigned over all Israel (2 Samuel 5:4,5).

God works in his time frame, not ours.

In fact, let this serve as an incentive to reignite your prayer life. What are your biggest fears, disappointments, and grievances? Start praying today for resolution, even a miracle.

There's one other account I want to look at that is pertinent to this topic. Matthew records the plight of another woman in a desperate circumstance. She wasn't asking for herself but on behalf of her daughter who was suffering terribly. So despite the fact that she was a non-Jew and Jesus was surrounded by men, she boldly went to him for help. Look at her story:

> **A Canaanite woman from that vicinity came to him, crying out, "Lord, Son of David, have mercy on me! My daughter is demon-possessed and suffering terribly."**
>
> **Jesus did not answer a word. So his disciples came to him and urged him, "Send her away, for she keeps crying out after us."**
>
> **He answered, "I was sent only to the lost sheep of Israel."**
>
> **The woman came and knelt before him. "Lord, help me!" she said.**
>
> **He replied, "It is not right to take the children's bread and toss it to the dogs."**
>
> **"Yes it is, Lord," she said. "Even the dogs eat the crumbs that fall from their master's table."**
>
> **Then Jesus said to her, "Woman, you have great**

faith! Your request is granted." And her daughter was healed at that moment. (Matthew 15:22–29)

This woman's cries went unheard and unanswered. Instead of receiving compassion, she was treated like a mosquito that needed a good swat. Her desperation did nothing to move Jesus to action. But she was unphased and undeterred. The disciples encouraged Jesus to send her away, but she came back. Jesus told her no, and she asked, "Why not?" He gave her a reason, and she appealed to God's mercy: "If the dogs get crumbs, then, Lord, I am more than good with that. Your crumbs, like the edge of your cloak and just three words from your mouth, can do infinitely more than anyone on earth can promise or provide."

How many of your prayers are in the dust bin of heaven because you are intimidated?

"You're right, Lord, I'm a lousy choice. I probably couldn't do that."

Says who?

"Well, this person hasn't given me a chance, and that opportunity didn't work out."

So what? Go back and ask for crumbs. Whatever that means in your case.

This woman didn't stop, and neither should you—not if what you're praying for is worth praying for. Are you praying for changed hearts and more people in heaven? Keep praying! Are you praying for more opportunities to share the gospel? Even if half of hell comes against you, keep praying!

Jesus himself said: **"Open your eyes and look at the fields! They are ripe for harvest"** (John 4:35).

Are you praying for healing, to overcome depression, to get past pain? Never give up. And never ever quit praying for your spouse, your children, your parents, your siblings, your church, your country.

Do not cower, and do not give up. Even when someone or many people scoff or laugh or tell you to give up. Nothing stopped that Canaanite woman, and nothing should stop you.

Jesus wasn't perturbed with her. He was astonished. "Woman, you have great faith!"

She believed impossible things could happen, and because of it, her impossible came true.

Do you have that kind of faith?

Three words, a touch of a cloak, and a few crumbs changed the lives of those who went to Jesus for help. It is not too much to go before God confidently and ask anything of him.

WHAT DOES THIS MEAN FOR YOU?

1. Do you believe God still does miracles? Why or why not?

2. The woman who was bleeding would not have been healed if she hadn't believed Jesus could do it. The Canaanite woman would not have gone home to a daughter in her right mind if she hadn't persisted. Read Mark 9:15–27. Think of what this father had been through. What led to the father's words in verse 22?

Jesus' words in verse 23 were a rebuke, not just for the man but also for you. How do you sabotage your impossible situations?

3. Let's get real for a minute. There are "impossibles" in all of our lives. To some degree, a lot of us have given up. We just accept these things as the way they are going to be and perhaps God *is* saying not now or maybe even no. But what if that isn't the case? The woman who bled for 12 years didn't stop trying to get help. The Canaanite woman didn't leave when Jesus didn't answer her the first or second time she called to him. So why do we? List your "impossibles" here:

4. Now how are you going to pray? Are you praying for total healing, for a turnaround, for a faith that doesn't waver, for God to fix this situation in even better ways than you can imagine?

CHAPTER 5

Confident to Put One Foot in Front of the Other as God Does the Work

Have you ever looked at a task in front of you and thought, *"Well, this may not be impossible, but it's close"*? In overwhelming situations, there are options.

Option 1: You can give up before you start and not try at all. When we're ready to admit it, a lot of us default to this option on a pretty regular basis, not just with the overwhelming things we should deal with but even with ambition to do other things. We should go through the storage area or stain the deck or go through the totes of pictures we inherited.

Maybe you're in over your head financially, but instead of taking steps to change it, you figure that's just the way it's going to be. Shrug. God must want you to stay broke. A relationship (with your boss, your spouse, a family member) is strained. It's frustrating and annoying, but what can you do?

Maybe you've always wanted to run a marathon but keep putting off training for it. (You can be sure this is not an aspiration of mine!)

Option 1 was played out in the Old Testament book of Numbers. Moses led the people of Israel to the border of Canaan. He sent 12 spies to explore the land. They came back with this report:

> **"We went into the land to which you sent us, and it does flow with milk and honey! Here is its fruit. But the people who live there are powerful, and the cities are fortified and very large. We even saw descendants of Anak there. The Amalekites live in the Negev; the Hittites, Jebusites and Amorites live in the hill country; and the Canaanites live near the sea and along the Jordan. . . . We can't attack those people; they are stronger than we are."** (Numbers 13:27–29,31)

The spies agreed it was a good land. But ten of them thought there was no use trying to take the land because the people were stronger. They gave up without giving it a chance, refused to trust God, and persisted in unbelief.

It is so easy to fall into this pattern. When you and I are faced with a health crisis or financial crisis or suddenly are without a job, a lot of times our brains default to, *"There's no way I'm getting through this!"* We mentally go through worst-case scenarios and shut down. When we do finally get around to acting, we look for the easiest, most comfortable option. We take that option and pretend it's all good.

Option 2: You work as if it all depends on you. You work two jobs and send text messages and seek the people out who are hurt and mad. You wear yourself out day after day. When you look around, you hope and pray you have the energy to keep going because if you don't, a lot will fall apart.

Moses was called to lead the people of Israel. Shortly after they left Egypt, as they were going through the desert, Moses' father-in-law, Jethro, came to visit him. When Jethro arrived, he observed this:

> **The next day Moses took his seat to serve as judge for the people, and they stood around him from morning till evening. When his father-in-law saw all that Moses was doing for the people, he said, "What is this you are doing for the people? Why do you alone sit as judge, while all these people stand around you from morning till evening?"**
>
> **Moses answered him, "Because the people come to me to seek God's will. Whenever they have a dispute, it is brought to me, and I decide between the parties and inform them of God's decrees and instructions."**

> **Moses' father-in-law replied, "What you are doing is not good. You and these people who come to you will only wear yourselves out. The work is too heavy for you; you cannot handle it alone. Listen now to me and I will give you some advice, and may God be with you. You must be the people's representative before God and bring their disputes to him. Teach them his decrees and instructions, and show them the way they are to live and how they are to behave. But select capable men from all the people—men who fear God, trustworthy men who hate dishonest gain—and appoint them as officials over thousands, hundreds, fifties and tens. Have them serve as judges for the people at all times, but have them bring every difficult case to you; the simple cases they can decide themselves. That will make your load lighter, because they will share it with you. If you do this and God so commands, you will be able to stand the strain, and all these people will go home satisfied."** (Exodus 18:13–23)

When Moses tried to do it all, he was overwhelmed. So were the people who had to wait all day to see him. You may find yourself in a similar situation. Yes, you can do it all, but who is getting the short end of the stick? Too often when you fall into this pattern, you give so much of your time and have nothing left to give to your family.

It's refreshing to read how Exodus chapter 18 continues:

> **Moses listened to his father-in-law and did everything he said. He chose capable men from all Israel and made them leaders of the people, officials over thousands, hundreds, fifties and tens. They served as judges for the people at all times. The difficult cases they brought to Moses, but the simple ones they decided themselves.** (verses 24-26)

Moses was carrying a weight he wasn't meant to carry. God didn't intend that he would do everything himself. Not only was it too much for him, but he was denying others the opportunity to use their gifts.

If you think you're the only one qualified to do something, there's a good chance you're on the road to burnout, and there's a better chance you have a problem with pride. Maybe initially you can do it better than someone else. That just means you need to train them and help them get to the point of being competent to do the work.

The more you put on yourself, the harder it is to do things well or to maintain a good attitude while doing it. If you're not careful, you'll eventually lose the excitement and joy of what you're doing and burn out, pulling a lot of people into a cyclone of grief and discontent as you go.

Option 3: You realize your strength is limited, but God's is not. This option means you submit to the fact that you are human and ask God to give you the strength to do what you need to do and the wisdom to know what you shouldn't be doing. When situations arise that require a whole lot more than you have to give, you don't shut down or rely on your own strength. Rather, you rely on God to get you through.

When the people of Israel began taking the land of Canaan, they were tricked into making a treaty with the Gibeonites. The Gibeonites saw what the Lord was doing through Israel. Fearing their destruction, they pretended to come from a long way away. The Israelites' leader at that time, Joshua, failed to inquire of the Lord, so he signed a treaty with the Gibeonites, only to find out they were inhabitants of Canaan.

Not long after the treaty was made, five kings from the area formed a coalition against Gibeon and attacked it. The king of Gibeon sent word to Joshua to come to their defense:

> **So Joshua marched up from Gilgal with his entire army, including all the best fighting men. The LORD said to Joshua, "Do not be afraid of them; I have given them into your hand. Not one of them will be able to withstand you."**
>
> **After an all-night march from Gilgal, Joshua took them by surprise. The LORD threw them into confusion before Israel, so Joshua and the Israelites defeated them completely at Gibeon. Israel pursued them along the road going up to Beth Horon and cut them down all the way to Azekah and Makkedah. As they fled before Israel on the road down from Beth Horon to Azekah, the LORD hurled**

large hailstones down on them, and more of them died from the hail than were killed by the swords of the Israelites.

On the day the Lord gave the Amorites over to Israel, Joshua said to the Lord in the presence of Israel:

"Sun, stand still over Gibeon, and you, moon, over the Valley of Aijalon." So the sun stood still, and the moon stopped, till the nation avenged itself on its enemies,

as it is written in the Book of Jashar.

The sun stopped in the middle of the sky and delayed going down about a full day. There has never been a day like it before or since, a day when the Lord listened to a human being. Surely the Lord was fighting for Israel!

Then Joshua returned with all Israel to the camp at Gilgal. (Joshua 10:7–15)

For better or worse, Joshua had given the Gibeonites his word. When they were attacked, he had to keep his promise.

It's easy to breeze past the details, but it's important to take the time to meditate on what happened. The men of

Israel began with an all-night march and then immediately engaged in battle. As the Lord routed the enemies, Joshua commanded the sun to stand still, and the sun did not set "for about a full day." I don't know, nor could I find an answer in the commentaries I consulted, if "a full day" was 12 or 24 hours.

Either way, the Israelite army marched, fought, and then marched home again in at least 48 hours, but possibly more. And during this time, God fought for and with the men of Israel. God promised to be with them and promised the enemy wouldn't stand. As Joshua and the men did what God commanded, God threw the enemy into confusion and hurled down hailstones, killing more men than the swords of the Israelites.

The men of Israel showed up, and God secured the victory. God did what they couldn't do on their own. God can and often will do the same thing for you. A lot of times you just need to ask for his help and then step out in faith to do the seemingly impossible things. Little by little, step by step, he helps you through.

Earlier this year I took a leadership class. Part of the curriculum was to study the spiritual gifts God gives to his people. I became enamored with the spiritual gift of faith. This gift is different than saving faith. Saving faith is knowing and believing that Jesus is your Savior. The spiritual gift of faith is "the ability to see something that needs to be done and believe that God will do it even if it looks impossible."[7]

If you've been around those who have the spiritual gift of faith, it's hard to ignore. These people are undeterred. No matter what comes into their lives, they know God is more than big enough to overcome the issue.

David (who would eventually become King David) had this gift. When he visited his brothers on a battlefield, he found them and the rest of the Israelite army **"dismayed and terrified"** (1 Samuel 17:11). A "champion" named Goliath, who stood nine feet nine inches, emerged every morning to taunt the Israelites. He challenged Israel to a fight, man against man, Goliath against whomever Israel chose. The winner's country would subjugate the loser's country.

God is more than big enough to overcome the issue.

When David went to King Saul to volunteer to fight Goliath, Saul responded, **"You are not able to go out against this Philistine and fight him; you are only a young man, and he has been a warrior from his youth"** (1 Samuel 17:33).

King Saul saw what David's brothers saw. David's faith was greater than his stature, physique, age, and every sane thought of every onlooker. In all of Israel, surely there was someone taller, stronger, more aggressive, better equipped.

But David's faith wasn't grounded in his ability, strength, or prowess. It was established in his identity as a child of God and God's ability to overcome what David couldn't on his own. Twice before God proved faithful: once when a lion attacked the flock David was watching and again when a bear did the same.

"The Lord who rescued me from the paw of the lion and the paw of the bear will rescue me from the hand of this Philistine," David said (1 Samuel 17:37).

And that's exactly what happened. The heavily armed Goliath fell. A stone from David's slingshot brought about his demise.

The book of Hebrews says it is impossible to please God without faith, because anyone who comes to him must believe that he exists and that he rewards those who earnestly seek him (11:6). This faith is **"confidence in what we hope for and assurance about what we do not see"** (Hebrews 11:1).

I don't know about you, but I want to please God, and it is impossible to do that when I don't think he's big enough to do what needs to be done. I can't please him when I refuse to see anything but the circumstances without allowing room for him to answer my prayers and take care of my "Goliaths" in ways I can't see.

Let that sink in.

To falter, to wonder, to doubt is to stand in unbelief. All of us stumble into that mentality or give the army of evil a little too much mental real estate at times. But like one man who brought his demon-possessed boy to Jesus, we can learn to recognize when we're falling into doubt and pray, **"I do believe; help me overcome my unbelief!"** (Mark 9:24). And that's the point of this chapter. You can never do it all, not based on your strength or ability or intelligence. But God working through and in you allows you to do far more than you could on your own.

Maybe you don't have the spiritual gift of faith. Maybe you are more of a realist, or you struggle to even imagine something is possible. Pray God gives you a friend with that gift so their eyes of faith can see what you can't. Pray that someone around you persuades you to believe things you never imagined could happen.

Throughout Scripture, God does the most impossible and improbable things in unlikely ways. When the people of Israel went into the Promised Land, the first town they came to and needed to conquer was Jericho.

According to archaeologists, Jericho was surrounded by an embankment with a stone retaining wall that was 12 to 15 feet high at its base. On top of the retaining wall was a mud-brick wall that was another 20 to 26 feet high. At the height of the embankment was a third mud-brick wall. "This is what loomed high above the Israelites as they marched around the city each day for seven days. Humanly speaking, it was impossible for the Israelites to penetrate the impregnable bastion of Jericho."[8]

And God's plan to get them through was not chinking away at it or using heavy artillery. It was a seven-day march, once around the city each day, followed by marching seven times around the city on the seventh day, then blaring trumpets, raising a shout, and watching the walls fall down.

It was an impossible task and an absurd solution. Who could or would take credit for that? The apostle Paul told the Corinthians, **"But God chose the foolish things of the**

world to shame the wise; God chose the weak things of the world to shame the strong" (1 Corinthians 1:27).

You don't have to worry that you aren't good enough to get the job done. If God only answered the prayers of the brightest and the best, most of us would be in trouble.

God just asks that you keep coming to him confidently and take the next step forward in faith, whatever that step is. If you ask anyone who has ever done anything how they did it, the answer is the same: One hundred pounds is lost one pound at a time. Writing a book is written one word, one paragraph, and one page at a time. You get out of a mess one good choice at a time, by the grace of God, and with the strength he provides.

God is not afraid of your impossible situations.

God is not afraid of your impossible situations, and he is never taken off guard. He stands ever present by your side and is more than equipped to handle anything you face. How silly if you deny him the opportunity to show his glory through you because you're worried or too weak. He knows you are, and it does not deter him. He's able and is well versed at helping the weak do more than they could ever do on their own.

WHAT DOES THIS MEAN FOR YOU?

1. The last time something unfortunate happened to me, my friends gathered around me, told me how big God is, and started praying bold prayers. If right now you are saying,

"Amber, I don't have that kind of friends," then let me assure you. I didn't either for many, many years! Several years ago, I started praying for strong Christian friends who would hold me accountable and teach me. God has been so generous in answering that prayer! In the meantime, if you don't have those people, turn your negatives into prayers. That job you hate is not the end. *God, open a door to a different job!* Your husband's bad attitude is no problem. *God, make him sweet and sensitive to my feelings!* It's a matter of changing the negatives into prayers. What negatives have come into your life in the past week?

How do those negatives lead you to pray?

2. Read Acts 5:40–42. How did the apostles pray after suffering persecution?

This puts your negatives in a totally different light. God doesn't have to give you a positive. He can bring glory out of shame, good out of pain. As you look at your list of negatives, how might you pray like the apostles in this part of the book of Acts?

CHAPTER 6

Confident God Won't Fail Even if You Do

In the Old Testament book of Judges, God reveals the account of Samson. Samson was a formidable opponent to Philistine oppression. From a spiritual standpoint, though, his life was more failure than success. And while it is not ideal to live a spiritually weak life, Samson's account is a reminder that when you call to God from the depths of despair, even when you've really messed things up, God hears you.

> **The angel of the LORD appeared to her and said, "You are barren and childless, but you are going to become pregnant and give birth to a son. Now see to it that you drink no wine or other fermented drink and that you do not eat anything unclean. You will become pregnant and have a son whose head is never to be touched by a razor because the boy is to be a Nazirite, dedicated to God from the**

womb. He will take the lead in delivering Israel from the hands of the Philistines." (Judges 13:3–5)

In Numbers chapter 6, God told Moses that a person could take a special vow of dedication to the Lord, known as a Nazarite vow. During the time of dedication, they were not to drink wine or any other fermented drink, eat anything that came from the grapevine (grapes or raisins), or cut their hair.

Whereas most people would take this vow for a specified time, Samson was to be a Nazarite for life. He was dedicated to the Lord to fulfill a specific purpose, namely, delivering Israel from the Philistines.

You might think that a child promised and set apart by God for a specific purpose would be nothing but a joy and delight. Scripture doesn't lead us to that conclusion. Time and again Samson's stubbornness and impulsiveness resulted in negative consequences for the people around him.

The first time was when Samson chose a wife. He saw a Philistine woman and told his father to get her for him. His father rightly responded: **"Isn't there an acceptable woman among your relatives or among all our people? Must you go to the uncircumcised Philistines to get a wife?"** (Judges 14:3).

God had commanded the people through Moses: **"Do not intermarry with** [the people of Canaan]**. Do not give your daughters to their sons or take their daughters for your sons, for they will turn your children away from following me to serve other gods, and the Lord's anger**

will burn against you and will quickly destroy you" (Deuteronomy 7:3,4).

But Samson wasn't having it. He saw the girl, wanted the girl, and commanded his father to get the girl. Once the marriage was arranged, Samson challenged the Philistines to solve a riddle. If they couldn't solve it, they would give him 30 linen garments and 30 sets of clothes, but if they did, he would give them 30 linen garments and 30 sets of clothes.

The Philistine men couldn't come up with the answer, so they coerced Samson's wife-to-be into getting the answer for them. Samson, knowing they cheated to get the answer, paid the debt by killing 30 Philistine men and stripping them of their clothes.

Not surprisingly, the woman's father gave the woman to another man to marry. When Samson found out, he caught 300 foxes, tied them together, and fastened torches to their tails. He lit the torches and burned the Philistines' grain fields, vineyards, and olive groves.

When the Philistines found out that Samson was responsible, they burned the woman and her father to death. Samson, in turn, slaughtered many Philistines.

Samson was insanely strong physically, but morally he was weak, especially when it came to women. The young Philistine woman was the first, then there was a prostitute, and eventually he fell in love with Delilah—who for a price, ultimately led to Samson's downfall.

Twice Delilah asked Samson what would cause him to lose his great strength, and twice he lied to her. Both times the Philistines did what he had told Delilah, and both times he escaped.

So why would he tell Delilah the terms of his Nazarite vow and expect anything different? Perhaps he took his strength for granted. He had grown used to having it and assumed he always would. Perhaps since he sinned sexually without noticeable consequence, he felt invincible.

There are times that you and I fail simply because it wasn't our time or because of circumstances outside of our control. But a lot of times, like Samson, our failure is a result of sin. When my husband and I are arguing, all too often I'm looking only at what I want or need and not paying attention to him or to God's command for wives to submit to their husbands (Ephesians 5:22). I don't want to submit, I don't feel like it, or I did last time.

Sometimes I fail at things because I want something but only put in a little bit of effort. My laziness is the disqualifying factor. Even when my failure is not a result of sin, sin is always a failure to take God's commands seriously.

Unrepented sin dulls our consciences.

Sometimes God is patient with us. He doesn't allow us to feel the consequences of our sin immediately. We can speed for months or years without getting a ticket. We can overeat day after day without dying of a heart attack. We can overspend and pick up extra hours at work to cover the cost of our purchases.

It's so easy to get comfortable in sin, but sin always

comes with a price. Unrepented sin dulls our consciences. We justify our actions. We pretend it's okay.

Psalm 66:18 says, **"If I had cherished sin in my heart, the Lord would not have listened."** To cherish is to protect or hold something dear. In this case, the something held dear is sin.

"The Lord would not have listened" is a daunting statement from a God who continually invites you and me to come to him with a statement like this: **"Ask and it will be given to you; seek and you will find; knock and the door will be opened to you"** (Matthew 7:7).

In the New Testament book of James, James wrote, **"If anyone, then, knows the good they ought to do and doesn't do it, it is sin for them"** (4:17). The apostle Paul encourages us to leave our wayward ways and live for Christ:

> **Do not let sin reign in your mortal body so that you obey its evil desires. Do not offer any part of yourself to sin as an instrument of wickedness, but rather offer yourselves to God as those who have been brought from death to life; and offer every part of yourself to him as an instrument of righteousness. For sin shall no longer be your master, because you are not under the law, but under grace.** (Romans 6:12-14)

Do not offer any part of yourself, not your mind allowing you to think about things you ought not to think about, not your hands considering doing things you aren't supposed to do (i.e., slapping the person talking to you), not your feet rushing into sin (rushing over to that person to talk about someone else).

Too often we ignore, refuse to deal with, or even embrace wrongdoing, and that's a dangerous path. Hebrews 3:7–11 says:

> **So, as the Holy Spirit says:**
>
> **"Today, if you hear his voice, do not harden your hearts as you did in the rebellion, during the time of testing in the wilderness, where your ancestors tested and tried me, though for forty years they saw what I did. That is why I was angry with that generation; I said, 'Their hearts are always going astray, and they have not known my ways.' So I declared on oath in my anger, 'They shall never enter my rest.'"**

God showed himself to the people of Israel time and again. He gave them a miraculous deliverance out of Egypt, where they had been slaves. He brought them to the edge of Canaan, where they refused to trust he would bring them into the land, so they were made to live in the desert for 40 years. During that time, God rained down food from heaven. He provided water when they were thirsty and meat when they complained. When enemies came against them, he delivered them. He did not allow their clothes or shoes to wear out, because they were in the desert and had no means to get more. Whatever they needed, he was faithful to supply. And yet when they came up against the next challenge, they chose to complain instead of trust.

God called it what it was: unbelief. The Israelites did not believe God was who he said he was. We don't want to fall into the same hardening of our hearts, refusing to turn from our sin or even take our sin seriously.

When Delilah shaved Samson's hair, the Nazarite vow was broken, and God left Samson. The man who had caused inconceivable damage to the Philistines for years was given into their hands. They gouged out his eyes, bound him, and made him grind grain in prison. Superman Samson became the laughingstock of the people he tormented.

The Philistines celebrated Samson's demise with a gathering to worship their god Dagon. Samson was brought out to perform for them. (We're not told how he performed or what that entailed.) When he was allowed to lean on the pillars that supported the temple, Samson asked God for strength just once more in order that he might push the supports over and destroy the temple. God gave him the strength he prayed for, and Samson died with all the others in the temple that day.

Samson didn't fall into moral failure; he dove in headfirst. Even when he was warned against it, he didn't listen, take heed, or slow down. He wanted what he wanted, and no one was going to keep him from getting it.

Call it what you want—your guilty pleasure, self-indulgence—it amounts to letting down your guard. James said, **"Each person is tempted when they are dragged away by their own evil desire and enticed"** (James 1:14).

Your uncontrolled and ill-thought-out desires drag you into all kinds of things you'd rather not do, and you are left to bear the consequences. When you're bored, frustrated, or worried, your desires easily drag you to those empty calories or to wasting time scrolling instead of praying or doing something of significance. The promise of the desire in the moment is satisfaction and calmed nerves. The consequences are extra pounds and living in the same rut because you gave in to your distractions instead of praying and seeing God's power unleashed in mighty ways.

And too often, an uncontrolled thought life allows lust unchecked. And that fantasy has you thinking about another person in ways your mind shouldn't, imagining a life of make-believe.

Desire can really mess with your emotions. Desire for attention, for self-worth, or to feel valued can drag you to the bottom of a very dark pit.

So much begins with a thought. That thought easily becomes desire, and desire has the power to taint your attitude, drive you to despair or to a thought life you wouldn't want anyone to see. And moral failure easily leads to familial strongholds and generational curses. The sins of your fathers easily become your sins and the sins you pass down to your children.

Samson's father tried to control his son by reminding him to look for a spouse among his own people. King David's servant tried to remind David, who was on a roof watching his neighbor Bathsheba taking a bath: **"She is Bathsheba, the daughter of Eliam and the wife of Uriah the Hittite"** (2 Samuel 11:3). "She's a daughter and a wife, David, someone you have no business looking at. Turn around; go back into the palace. Spend time with one of your wives."

If you don't have people like that in your life, it's worth praying God would supply them. *"Give me friends and mentors to hold me accountable, Lord. And give me a humble heart to listen when they warn me that I'm going the wrong way!"*

Whether you tiptoe over it or blatantly overlook a boundary, it's all too easy to slip. And if you don't get up immediately, run to God's grace, and ask for his help and the help of others, it's so easy to stay in that cycle of sin. And once you're in that pit, it's easy to sink into thinking you can never get out or to convince yourself that it doesn't matter. *"God doesn't care about a little gossip or me embellishing the story a little. He certainly doesn't mind that I drink too much, eat too much, or can't tell my husband the truth about what I spent."*

Except that he does.

Jesus said all kinds of hard things, not the least of which was to **"be perfect, therefore, as your heavenly Father is perfect"** (Matthew 5:48).

This statement came after a whole bunch of difficult teachings:

> **"Give to the one who asks you, and do not turn away from the one who wants to borrow from you.**
>
> **"You have heard that it was said, 'Love your neighbor and hate your enemy.' But I tell you, love your enemies and pray for those who persecute you, that you may be children of your Father in heaven. He causes his sun to rise on the evil and the good, and sends rain on the righteous and the unrighteous. If you love those who love you, what reward will you get? Are not even the tax collectors doing that? And if you greet only your own people, what are you doing more than others? Do not even pagans do that? Be perfect, therefore, as your heavenly Father is perfect."** (Matthew 5:42–48)

Give your stuff away. Love people who hate you and treat you unfairly. Pray for people who make your life miserable. Be perfect.

Easy, right?

Hardly.

But it's far easier to take Jesus' words seriously than to live with the fallout from living in sin. Feeling like a failure is only part of the problem. That gossip will never bring you the close friendships you crave. Becoming a trustworthy person will. When people know they can trust you, they share their hearts freely and you in turn can walk with them through the hardest, stormiest days of their lives.

And holding a grudge doesn't help you heal, no matter how bad they were or how bad it hurt. Praying for your persecutors does though. The note in my study Bible says, "We can and should pray that they will repent or relent. We want them to see the error of their ways, seek God's forgiveness, and obtain eternal life."[9]

Sin promises so much but delivers only temporary pleasure. You can eat another piece of chocolate or try another glass of wine or fantasize about a different future, but day after day and night after night they leave you coming back to be filled again.

And so will all your stuff. No matter how many things you bring into the house or how fun it is to pick it out and imagine the value it will add, the truth is so sneaky. Most of your stuff takes more than it gives. It takes your money, your time, your attention, and your effort. And before long you're looking at the next thing, thinking maybe it will make your life just right.

The opposite is true. Jesus said, **"It is more blessed to give than to receive"** (Acts 20:35). Squandering your money on things that don't last is the devil's way of keeping you from investing in the things that do.

Instead of craving what the world doesn't give, be perfect. That's a tall order for sinners. "Christ sets up the high ideal of perfect love—not that we can fully attain it in this life. That, however, is God's high standard for us."[10]

Just ask Adam and Eve how easy it is to live up to God's standard. They had an entire garden of perfect fruit. There was just one tree they weren't supposed to eat from. One. And what did they do? They craved the fruit of the one tree, neglecting all the other great fruit they were allowed to eat.

Samson walked right into sin. Many Jesus followers try to avoid it. Even so, they fail again and again.

There's a difference between trying to do the right thing but failing and embracing sin. As hard as you try to do what is right, you fail all the time, and God's grace meets you every time you do. You don't achieve all you'd like; you do stupid stuff you don't want to do. You don't do the stuff you should. But God continues to show up and continues to work through you in spite of you.

God continues to show up.

You are going to fail. The key is to get back up! The lessons you learn when you fail help develop a dependency on God. You can't do life alone. It's much better to realize your weaknesses, take control of your thoughts, walk with people who hold you accountable, and know it is only God in you who achieves anything. Then with the apostle Paul you can rightfully admit:

> **God chose the lowly things of this world and the despised things—and the things that are not—to nullify the things that are, so that no one may boast before him. It is because of him that you are in Christ Jesus, who has become for us wisdom from God—that is, our righteousness, holiness and redemption. Therefore, as it is written: "Let**

the one who boasts boast in the Lord."
(1 Corinthians 1:28–31)

Every good thing you do is God working through you. And if you let him, God can and does take your failures and turns them into something worthwhile too.

Romans 8:28 says, **"And we know that in all things God works for the good of those who love him, who have been called according to his purpose."** The note in my NIV study Bible says, "The good: that which conforms us 'to the likeness of his Son.'"[11]

You don't always see God working for your good because you are looking for the easiest route filled with the greatest material blessings. But God is looking at your heart, and his goal is to make you more like Jesus. Failure is good when you learn humility. It's good when it keeps you from things that would make you more invested in the world and less on fire for God's kingdom. It's good when it brings the people around you to realize that life on this earth is temporary but eternity stands before you. And it's good if it sifts people out of your life who don't have in mind the things of God.

God worked for good in Samson's failure. At the end of his life, Samson turned back to God. Satan and his evil army would love to keep you stuck and wallowing and thinking God can't use you because you're too far gone.

That's not how God sees you. **"For you are a people holy to the LORD your God. The LORD your God has chosen you**

out of all the peoples on the face of the earth to be his people, his treasured possession" (Deuteronomy 7:6).

Don't let failure define you. You are God's holy, chosen, treasured possession, whether you win or lose, look great or frumpy, rise to the top or remain faithful at the bottom. No one but God has the power or authority to define you.

What now? First, realize you are not a lost cause. Second, know there is hope. Change happens one decision at a time, and the first decision you need to make is to bring God into the equation.

God can turn things around in your life. Pray he gives you the strength to make the next good choice. Pray he shows you how to do life differently if you feel more failure than joy. Pray he puts people in your life to lift you up and teach you and mentor you to live differently. Pray he helps you to demolish every thought that comes into your head that is not in accordance to his Word and will.

Whatever you have been or thought you were in the past is irrelevant. Let God define you. Let his Word be the last and only word that matters to you. Then get back up confidently. This is your time to tell people about Jesus and let your testimony shine as a beacon of the hope you have in him.

WHAT DOES THIS MEAN FOR YOU?

1. All too often you and I look at the end goal instead of the journey. And sometimes when we only see the big goal at the end, it seems too big to achieve, so we throw in the

towel. What small steps in your life would lead to overcoming the sin you're struggling with? Let me get you started with a few ideas.

a. Talk to someone about your struggle.

b. Find a book or podcast that addresses what you are trying to overcome.

c.

d.

e.

2. Sometimes you don't know what steps to take, and that's the problem! Look up James 4:7. *Resist* means "to withstand or to refrain from doing something." If a friend calls and asks you to go out when you're trying to avoid drinking, resisting looks like saying: "No. I'm going to stay home tonight." When an ugly thought comes into your mind, Satan or one of his minions is saying, "Come on, let's go." What does resisting temptation look and sound like?

3. Sometimes you just need to be reminded that failing doesn't make you a failure. Write out Romans 8:37.

   Now personalize it. "In God, I am not a victim. I'm a conqueror. In fact, I am more than a conqueror." How does a victim respond to things not going as planned or working out versus how a conqueror would respond?

CHAPTER 7

Confident That Difficult People Are No Problem for God

This is not one of my favorite subjects. To me, it's easy. Difficult people should just stop being difficult. Unless, of course, you and I are the difficult ones. Then, well, may God show us our sin and turn our hearts back to him!

The book of Daniel begins with Daniel, Shadrach, Meshach, and Abednego being taken in the first wave of captives from Judah to serve in King Nebuchadnezzar's court in Babylon. They were given new names, put through a rigorous educational and training period, and had to defend their desire to eat according to their Jewish customs instead of eating the food dedicated to idols.

By the second chapter of Daniel, we get a glimpse into the kind of person King Nebuchadnezzar was. He had a dream, and rather than tell his wise men the dream, he insisted the wise men tell him the dream and its interpretation because he feared the wise men would simply make up an explanation to sound good. When they told him it was impossible, Nebuchadnezzar ordered they all be put to death. Sounds like a difficult person to me! Maybe there was an abundance of wise men in Babylon at the time. Maybe Nebuchadnezzar figured he'd be better on his own or heard one too many lousy interpretations.

At any rate, that's how an executioner ended up on Daniel's doorstep. I'm not sure how I would have responded to an executioner showing up at my house, but Daniel struck up a conversation. Once he knew the situation, he asked to be taken to the king to ask for time. The king granted his request, and Daniel and his friends began praying to know the dream and its interpretation.

The book of Daniel teaches many lessons, not the least of which is to turn to God when you have an impossible person in your life. You may never have to deal with someone determining what food you can eat or if you will live or die, but people can make your life pretty miserable just the same.

And all too often, it's not a situation you can walk away from. If that person is part of your family, you may have to deal with them at holidays or special events. Moving might not be an option when a new neighbor buys the house next door. And what do you do when you love your job but your boss retires and the new guy is not your biggest fan?

Daniel, Shadrach, Meshach, and Abednego couldn't leave Babylon, and it's not like they had rights as captives. They were stuck dealing with Nebuchadnezzar. Even after

Daniel told Nebuchadnezzar about the dream, the King's newfound awe of Daniel's God didn't last long.

This is not a surprise to anyone who has prayed for an unbelieving friend or family member for any amount of time. They get sick. You pray. God heals them. Things go back to status quo until the next crisis when you pray, God shows up, and you point out God's gracious answer to prayer. Repeat. Thank God for his patience.

Soon after the dream incident, Nebuchadnezzar set up a huge golden statue, gathered all his administrators and employees, and ordered them to bow down and worship it. Shadrach, Meshach, and Abednego refused, and Nebuchadnezzar had them thrown into a furnace hot enough to kill the soldiers who threw them in. God spared their lives and even sent an angel who appeared with them in the furnace. When they came out, their clothes were intact; their hair wasn't singed. They didn't even smell like smoke!

Surely that made an impression on Nebuchadnezzar! But reading the next three chapters of the book of Daniel is a reminder that Daniel would serve pagan leaders the rest of his days and would often find himself as the odd man out.

Following God is like that a lot of times. Sometimes you are the only Christian in your workplace. Some people become Christians after they marry and suddenly find themselves in a difficult position with someone who doesn't believe the way they do. There's plenty of struggle even in Christian homes: with addiction, mental health, physical health, old age, with children who stray. All too often these things cause the people you do life with to be less than fun to be around. What can you do in those situations?

When Daniel and his friends came to a new challenge, they got creative. They sought an exemption with the diet and were willing to undergo a short-term trial to prove it would work. When the executioner came knocking on Daniel's door, Daniel spoke to him with wisdom and tact. He convinced the executioner it would be worth it to take him to the king. When Shadrach, Meshach, and Abednego were given an ultimatum to bow down to the statue or be thrown into the furnace, they clearly but respectfully stated their allegiance to God.

All those things point to the fruit of a mature spiritual walk with God. To remain calm in the storms, to be kind even when confronted by a hothead, and to state fearlessly that following God is worth more than life itself are not automatic behaviors but behaviors that are refined through Bible study and prayer.

But there's another lesson too important to miss. Daniel had a healthy dependency on prayer as a means of communicating his needs to God. After the executioner took him to see the king: **"Then Daniel returned to his house and explained the matter to his friends Hananiah, Mishael and Azariah** [also named Shadrach, Meshach, and Abednego]**. He urged them to plead for mercy from the God of heaven concerning this mystery, so that he and his friends might not be executed with the rest of the wise men of Babylon"** (Daniel 2:17,18).

In Daniel chapter 6, after a different king made an edict that anyone who prayed to anyone but him for 30 days would be thrown into a lions' den, it says:

> **Now when Daniel learned that the decree had been published, he went home to his upstairs room where the windows opened toward Jerusalem. Three times a day he got down on his knees and prayed, giving thanks to his God, just as he had done before. Then these men went as a group and found Daniel praying and asking God for help.** (verses 10,11)

In Daniel chapter 10, Daniel saw a vision of a man:

> **He said, "Daniel, you who are highly esteemed, consider carefully the words I am about to speak to you, and stand up, for I have now been sent to you." And when he said this to me, I stood up trembling.**
>
> **Then he continued, "Do not be afraid, Daniel. Since the first day that you set your mind to gain understanding and to humble yourself before your God, your words were heard, and I have come in response to them."** (verses 11,12)

Daniel, according to the man, set his mind to gain

understanding, humbled himself before God, and prayed. If you are in a struggle right now with a difficult person, this seems like a pretty good game plan for coping. *"God, help me to understand where this person's negativity is coming from. Is there unresolved hurt or shame? God, I don't understand, and I don't have answers, but I know you see and understand all things. Show me what to do, when to speak, and when to listen. Help me!"*

I've studied the book of Esther more than a few times, and Esther had to deal with some difficult people too.

The first thing to note when reading this book are the characteristics of King Xerxes. In the opening chapter, he had a six-month party to show off his wealth. He summoned his wife to his banquet, where the alcohol was abundant, in order that he might show off her beauty to a group of men. And when she refused, he relieved her of her position as queen.

Daniel humbled himself before God and prayed.

I don't know about you, but that doesn't put Xerxes in line for husband of the year in my book, but then again, I've never been in charge of an empire with that kind of power at my disposal. My impression of him only gets worse as he goes along with his advisors' plan to bring all the beautiful young virgins of the land to his harem and give them beauty treatments for a year before being taken to the king. The note in my NIV study Bible says, "Esther also was taken. Neither she nor Mordecai would have had any choice in the matter."[12] The EHV study Bible says something quite different. It states: "Esther is among the candidates who are auditioned for the position of queen. The text does not state whether she volunteered or was drafted. She seems to be a willing participant in the sordid process, but according to Herodotus many unwilling women were forced into Xerxes' net. Esther may be one of them. At any rate Esther agrees to hide her faith. In this regard she is a stark contrast to Daniel and his friends. This is one of the reasons some readers were uncomfortable with the book of Esther. Be that as it may, the Lord will make use of Esther's secrecy to undo Haman."[13]

As much as I have enjoyed my EHV Bible, I abhor the word *audition* used in this context for a few reasons. First, the fact that Mordecai determined and Esther obeyed him in terms of keeping her Jewish identity a secret does not in my opinion make her a willing participant. It makes her what Jesus called shrewd as a snake (Matthew 10:16). By that I mean she hid in plain sight, blended in, kept her head down, and didn't make waves. But mostly I abhor it because of what comes next:

> **And this is how she would go to the king: Anything she wanted was given her to take with her from the harem to the king's palace. In the evening she would go there and in the morning return to another part of the harem to the care of Shaashgaz, the king's eunuch who was in charge of the concubines. She would not return to the king unless he was pleased with her and summoned her by name.** (Esther 2:13,14)

The indication is that the virgin did not return as a virgin. I wouldn't call what transpired an audition in any circumstance. Esther may not have protested, but that doesn't mean she agreed with what took place. She may not have had the courage of Shadrach, Meshach, and Abednego who refused to bow down to Nebuchadnezzar's idol, but that, in my opinion, does not equate to acquiescence. It may simply mean that Mordecai and Esther knew Xerxes' character and knew he was not a man to mess with. Any noncompliance on her part would likely have resulted in death, and rather than go that route, she chose to comply.

In the book of 2 Kings, we see a similar situation. A man named Naaman, who had leprosy, came from Aram to see God's prophet Elisha to be healed. Elisha gave Naaman directions to wash in the Jordan River. When he did, Naaman was healed of his leprosy. Once he was healed, Naaman confessed, **"Now I know that there is no God in all the world except in Israel"** (2 Kings 5:15).

Naaman understood that this newfound faith would put him in a difficult position when he returned home, so he said to Elisha: **"'But may the Lord forgive your servant for this one thing: When my master enters the temple of Rimmon to bow down and he is leaning on my arm and I have to bow there also—when I bow down in the temple of Rimmon, may the Lord forgive your servant for this.' 'Go in peace,' Elisha said"** (2 Kings 5:18,19).

Naaman no longer wanted to kneel before another god. He now knew the true God, who had healed him. Naaman asked to be forgiven for bowing with his master, and Elisha granted him freedom of conscience.

Many women in China were forced to have abortions during the time when each family was allowed to have only one child. It was not their idea, nor did they feel as if they had a choice. Would God have provided miraculously if a woman had a child secretly? Possibly he would have, but that would have meant she would have to hide her pregnancy and quite possibly give birth outside of a hospital. Where would the child go to school? Could she hide said child for life? Many women didn't see that as an option. God will hold the leaders of China responsible for the blood of those children.

Is it easy to pretend that you would make a different decision if in that situation? And maybe you would. Sin is never the preferred option. But God's mercy forgives even the sins you commit when you aren't courageous enough to stand up to do what is right because you cower.

Would Esther have rather had the traditional Jewish marriage? Did she and Mordecai willingly go along with Xerxes' plan with the hopes that she would become queen? I can't answer either of those questions. I can't imagine wanting to be married to Xerxes knowing what she knew, but that too is not a sentiment I can make with any certainty.

Soon after Esther's marriage, Mordecai uncovered a plot to assassinate Xerxes, told Esther, and saved Xerxes' life. Xerxes made a man named Haman his right-hand man, and for whatever reason, Mordecai was not a fan of Haman. Mordecai alone refused to bow to Haman.

Again, the Bible doesn't give context, only facts. The king ordered that everyone bow to Haman, and Mordecai refused. In retaliation, Haman sought not only to destroy Mordecai but every Jew. And somehow, in a conversation that lasted less than most sitcoms, Haman convinced Xerxes to go along with his plan. The fate of the Jews was set, and the proclamation was sent out.

If the first chapters of the book of Esther show Xerxes to be arrogant, extravagant, prone to rash decisions, and an excessive drinker, this turn of events doesn't do much to color his character in a positive light. Esther's reaction when called upon to approach him for help shows their relationship wasn't like marriages today. She knew the law, and the law was that she couldn't go to him unless called. She had not been called in a month.

Add to that the fact that Haman was also arrogant, rash, power-hungry, and influential with Xerxes, and Esther had her hands full.

The book of Esther shows that difficult, rash, powerful, arrogant, influential people are no trouble for God. In perhaps the most entertaining turn of events in the Bible, Haman met his demise even as he plotted to bring down Mordecai.

Christians don't need to fret when seemingly the wrong person comes into a position of authority or a place to influence their lives negatively. They don't need to go about wringing their hands or complaining to whoever will listen.

Proverbs 21:1 states, **"In the Lord's hand the king's**

heart is a stream of water that he channels toward all who please him." If God can direct the heart of a king, he certainly can change the heart of your spouse or neighbor or whoever makes your life difficult.

When we were married, my husband, Steve, and I moved into a house that shared a driveway with another house. A beautiful elderly couple owned the other house. They taught us everything about being good neighbors. When our water heater needed to be replaced, the gentleman taught Steve to do it. When our birthdays or anniversary came around, they were at our door with cookies and a card. For many, many years, our children wandered over to the "old folks' house," as our neighbors liked to call it, to check in with and entertain them.

As the years passed, the gentleman began caring for his wife who struggled with dementia. As his caretaking duties increased, so did his irritability. He suddenly started finding everything our children did annoying. Every time I saw him walking down the driveway, my heart sank because I knew he had another complaint.

Early on Steve and I decided we would love him no matter what. I'd thank him for letting me know about the latest complaint, and I'd give him a hug. More than once when I hugged the man, tears fell from his eyes.

God was the only one who could give us the strength to return his complaints with loving-kindness. By doing so, our relationship was kept intact, and that led to a time when I would take care of him in the last year of his life.

Jesus told us to **"love your enemies and pray for those who persecute you"** (Matthew 5:44). He went on to say there would be a reward. You can't begin to know what that reward is at the time, but there will be a reward. Sometimes it is the reward of a relationship. Sometimes it is seeing someone come to faith. For Esther and Mordecai, it was the deliverance of their people.

If you were to question if Mordecai's stubbornness was the catalyst for causing the situation and raise the possibility of his being somewhat difficult, you may not be entirely wrong. If only we knew the whole story. We don't. We know what God allows us to know. But that possibility leads us back to the way I began this chapter.

Sometimes you and I are the difficult ones. We may think we are right or justify what we do, but we can't neglect the apostle Paul's words in 1 Corinthians 13:1–3:

> **If I speak in the tongues of men or of angels, but do not have love, I am only a resounding gong or a clanging cymbal. If I have the gift of prophecy and can fathom all mysteries and all knowledge, and if I have a faith that can move mountains, but do not have love, I am nothing. If I give all I possess to the poor and give over my body to hardship that I may boast, but do not have love, I gain nothing.**

We do a lot of damage; in fact, we use God's name in vain when we act selfishly or abusively or hardhearted toward others while professing to be Christians. Doing so tarnishes God's good name and may keep people from wanting to be Christians.

We don't love perfectly all the time, but it's certainly worth considering and asking God and the people around us how we can improve our disposition if this is our struggle.

God doesn't expect us to do this on our own or by our own strength. God will strengthen us and help us (Isaiah 41:10), especially when we ask him to do so.

When my son was 15, he asked me if I had anything positive to say to him. That statement changed my parenting. I didn't realize until that moment that most of my communication sounded like this: "Did you shut the garage door? Put your shoes away. Make sure to . . ."

I started trying to catch my kids doing something praiseworthy. I tried to remember to thank them. I slowly and deliberately started building them up with my words instead of complaining or reminding them of something they didn't do.

I am still working on it seven years later, but I'm a whole lot better than I was, and I'm committed to being better, not just with my children but in general.

I don't think most of us want to be difficult. A whole lot of times we don't realize that we are. But are we encouraging? Are we grateful? Are we kind?

God forgives us every time we mess up. With his help and the strength he provides, we can do better. It's amazing how relationships change when we are.

WHAT DOES THIS MEAN FOR YOU?

1. List the qualities that make a person difficult to live with or next to or work with or worship with.

2. How many of those qualities do you possess?

3. The Pharisees at Jesus' time thought they were right and their way was the only way. They were self-righteous, justifying their actions and the reasons for living as they did. All too often, that's how we get stuck in unloving patterns. We put God in a box of our imagination: This is the way to do church. This is the way to worship. This is the only way our family is going to function. On several occasions, Jesus discredited the Pharisees and told them they were way off base. On one occasion, the apostle Paul confronted Peter when he was wrong. The apostle Paul and Barnabas got into a heated argument about who should go on a missionary journey. Who holds you accountable if you're being unloving, rigid, and unkind?

4. Some of us can be perfectly loving to our believing friends but judgmental of anyone outside the church. Read 1 Corinthians 5:12 and 2 Corinthians 4:4. How do these passages challenge you to treat unbelievers in a kind and loving way?

CHAPTER 8

Confident God Works Through Your Suffering

If I'm honest, I don't always want the strength to endure. I just want the bad stuff to go away. I want peace, health, and easy living. But today a friend I get to see once a year reminded me of the importance of suffering. That's how many of the best lessons are learned.

Consider the prophet Jonah from the Bible. God gave him an explicit assignment to preach in Nineveh. But Jonah didn't want to go to Nineveh, so instead of following God's command, he caught the first ship in the opposite direction.

God could have chosen another prophet. He could have let Jonah continue in disobedience. But he didn't. He sent a violent storm, and despite the efforts of the crew, nothing helped until they took Jonah's advice and threw him overboard.

That could have been the end of Jonah. God could have allowed him to drown. But he didn't. He caused a big fish to swallow Jonah. And he let Jonah think for at least a part of the next three days. From inside the fish, Jonah confessed that God heard his prayer and rescued him. Jonah thanked the Lord and promised to do the work God wanted him to do.

That's a pretty significant turnaround. I'd love to think Jonah might have had a change of heart an easier way than getting thrown overboard, nearly drowning, and being stuck in the belly of a fish, but God knew exactly what it would take.

The apostle Paul started his adult life as a Pharisee who zealously persecuted the Christian church, even approving of the imprisonment and brutal death of believers. God appeared to him and struck him with blindness, and that got his attention as the Holy Spirit turned Paul from disobedience to belief.

You and I ought to pray for similar wake-up calls! The longer we wallow in disobedience, the more our consciences dull to sin.

When my kids entered their teen years, I started praying God would stop all of us in our tracks and bring us back if we were wandering into sin. At the time we had a dog, so I prayed God would keep us on a short leash in order that we might stay close to him.

God can use those uncomfortable, scary times not only to turn us from sin but sometimes to redirect our course. For the reformer Martin Luther, a violent thunderstorm threatened his life, and he promised God if he were to live, he would become a monk. That promise was the beginning of his careful study of the Scriptures that weren't widely available to anyone outside of the priesthood in those days.

That in turn resulted in his discovery of the concept of grace, which led to his efforts toward reformation.

For me it was an emergency landing followed by two sketchy flights to Asia. I had been living as a college student with worldly goals. I was in my early 20s and not living a right life in many respects. When that plane turned around because it was leaking fuel, I was filled with dread. While I walked laps around LAX airport throughout the night, I prayed, *"Spare my life, Lord, and I will serve you."*

That is not to suggest that every time someone suffers God is trying to get their attention, turn them from disobedience, or redirect them to a different path for their life. Jesus suffered, and he obeyed perfectly and always did exactly what his heavenly Father desired. The writer of Hebrews says, **"During the days of Jesus' life on earth, he offered up prayers and petitions with fervent cries and tears to the one who could save him from death, and he was heard because of his reverent submission. Son though he was, he learned obedience from what he suffered and, once made perfect, he became the source of eternal salvation for all who obey him"** (5:7–9).

In the Garden of Gethsemane, Jesus asked the Father if there was an alternative way for him to save us. Jesus knew what was ahead: the cruel mockery, beating, whipping, humiliation, torture, and death. But that was not what troubled Jesus. On the cross, the Father turned away from him as Jesus paid the debt of all the world's sins.

The Father's answer was no, but he didn't leave Jesus

empty-handed. He equipped him to meet this challenge—an angel strengthened Jesus' resolve for the task ahead.

My Bible's note on Hebrews chapter 5 says, "Though he was the eternal Son of God, it was necessary for him as the incarnate Son to learn obedience—not that he was ever disobedient, but that he was called on to obey to an extent he had never before experienced. The temptations he faced were real and the battle for victory was difficult, but where Adam failed and fell, Jesus resisted and prevailed. His humanity was thereby completed; 'made perfect', and on the basis of this perfection he could become 'the source of eternal salvation.'"[14]

Jesus endured through suffering and prevailed. Thankfully, you won't have to endure anything even close to what Jesus went through, but you can look to Jesus' example to remind you

- that God sees and hears you in your suffering.
- that even when he allows you to suffer, he often provides you with strength and sustenance while you endure.
- that God promises you that good will come from whatever you go through. Romans 8:28 assures you God doesn't allow you to suffer without a plan to use it somehow and in some way.
- that if Jesus, the sinless Son of God, suffered while he was on earth, why do you think you shouldn't have to?

Most of the time, I want the easiest and fastest, without desiring the best. To be mature Christians, we need to learn to persevere and endure. James said this: **"Consider it pure joy, my brothers and sisters, whenever you face trials of many kinds, because you know that the testing of your faith produces perseverance. Let perseverance finish its work so that you may be mature and complete, not lacking anything"** (James 1:2-4).

We need to learn to persevere and endure.

You persevere when you worship through the hard times, when you keep trusting even though you don't see an answer to your prayers. And as you do this, you are becoming a stable, mature, refined Christian who doesn't easily bend or break. Suffering builds your spiritual muscles.

The apostle Paul said in 2 Corinthians 1:8-11:

> **We do not want you to be uninformed, brothers and sisters, about the troubles we experienced in the province of Asia. We were under great pressure, far beyond our ability to endure, so that we despaired of life itself. Indeed, we felt we had received the sentence of death. But this happened that we might not rely on ourselves but on God, who raises the dead. He has delivered us from such a deadly peril, and he will deliver us again. On him we have set our hope that he will continue to deliver us, as you help us by your prayers.**

Paul and his companions despaired of life, but they learned to rely on God. The next time they had to suffer, they wouldn't so easily despair. God delivered them before. And one way or another, he would deliver them again.

The question then is, How do you endure during the suffering however long it lasts? The most beautiful people I've known are the ones who are not in the best circumstances, but you wouldn't know it by their attitudes. They have learned to be people who **"do everything without grumbling or arguing"** (Philippians 2:14).

The first man I ever cared for as a private elderly companion was a retired pastor who could no longer speak. He was in a nursing home and dependent on people to do everything for him. The way he communicated most was through his smile. He endeared himself to everyone with that one simple expression.

When I went to see a dear friend in the hospital two days before she died of cancer, she made me feel like I was the greatest person to walk the earth because I had come to see her.

Job became an example for us all when he lost everything in one day and fell to the ground worshiping, saying, **"Naked I came from my mother's womb, and naked I will depart. The Lord gave and the Lord has taken away; may the name of the Lord be praised"** (Job 1:21).

And then there's Abraham. Genesis chapter 22 presents the account of God asking Abraham to sacrifice his son Isaac. Abraham had waited 25 years and was 100 years old when he had his son Isaac. God reassured him that the Savior would come through Isaac (Genesis 17:21). It made no sense for God to ask Abraham to offer Isaac as a burnt offering.

And yet early the next day, Abraham, Isaac, and two servants set out on a three-day journey to Mount Moriah, where God commanded them to go.

When Abraham saw the place in the distance, he told his servants: **"Stay here with the donkey while I and the boy go over there. We will worship and then we will come back to you"** (Genesis 22:5).

One commentary notes that Abraham's words, "we will worship," are a declaration that God had Abraham's heart, and the Hebrew word for "we will come back" is an emphatic verb expressing determination.[15]

Abraham was determined to obey and to worship even if it meant giving up his only son. Could you worship through suffering and obey if it meant great sacrifice?

Abraham knew God's character, and that allowed him to trust and not doubt. The writer of Hebrews explains:

> **By faith Abraham, when God tested him, offered Isaac as a sacrifice. He who had embraced the promises was about to sacrifice his one and only son, even though God had said to him, "It is through Isaac that your offspring will be reckoned." Abraham reasoned that God could even raise the dead, and so in a manner of speaking he did receive Isaac back from death.** (11:17–19)

Whatever suffering you endure, you can trust God has it under control. If you aren't being delivered, then surely he will give you strength. Quite possibly, God hasn't rescued you because there's still more to learn, if not for you then for someone near and dear to you. Or maybe God is putting you in places you'd never be if it weren't for the suffering.

Many Christians around the world are put in jails and prisons each year, and while there, they tell other prisoners about God. People's eternal destinies change because of the suffering of those saints.

You can trust God has it under control.

Other times God uses suffering as a means for others to serve you and me. Twice while I had pneumonia during my fourth pregnancy, a neighbor I barely knew stopped over with food for my family. I was so thankful for that woman.

God's ways are good, even when you don't understand. Nothing you go through lasts forever. God knows when it's time to act, when deliverance must come, and when it's time to take you home.

You can trust and be confident that God has a plan for your life.

WHAT DOES THIS MEAN FOR YOU?

1. Last night I received a text from a friend. Her friend's daughter had committed suicide. From a human perspective, I can't see good. My prayers sound like this: *"God, you can make good come from bad. I don't understand.*

Help. Give the parents strength to endure this. Holy Spirit, intervene because I don't know how to pray, but I know you do and will on my behalf." Look up Philippians 4:6,7. What does Paul teach about obtaining comfort in crisis?

2. Read Matthew 11:28–30. Weary means feeling exhaustion. Burdened is to be carrying a load. In these verses, Jesus says his yoke is easy and his burden is light. Jesus says he will carry what you can't. The situation I described in #1 would fit into something too hard to handle. How does this passage teach you to pray during times of suffering?

3. Read Romans 5:3–5. There's always more to learn. How does this passage lead you to pray in order that you come out on the other side of suffering a person who is more prepared to serve in God's kingdom?

4. Read Romans 12:15. What tangible things can you do when it's your friends who are suffering and not you?

5. Who in your life is struggling right now? What can you do to help?

CHAPTER 9

Confident You Don't Need More

I need to start this chapter with a disclaimer. Both my husband and I have had a little experience this year cleaning out relatives' houses. If you've never gone through a person's house after they've moved to a nursing home, died, or because they were in the process of downsizing to go to a senior living facility, you may not comprehend just how much people tend to accumulate. Spend a day or a few weeks or months doing it, and you will have a new appreciation for how many useless things we spend our hard-earned money on. And when you finish, if in fact you do, you may have a new appreciation for minimalism.

My goals last year included being less greedy and more generous. Greed is a selfish desire for something, especially wealth, power, or food. If you were to dig into my life, you might not think I'm greedy. Our house and cars are pretty modest. I usually thrift for my clothes. We don't eat out a lot. We give to our church and other charities and ministries.

But I couldn't get rid of this nagging feeling that all things considered, we really weren't giving that much. Here's what I mean. According to the world bank:

- 8.5 percent of the global population—almost 700 million people—live today on less than $2.15 per day, the extreme poverty line relevant for low-income countries.
- 44 percent of the global population—around 3.5 billion people—live today on less than $6.85 per day, the poverty line relevant for upper middle-income countries.[16]

That means that half of the people on earth live on less than seven dollars a day. In every one of those people's eyes, I would be considered a person of substantial wealth.

It's easy to get lost in the "more" mentality. If I'm having people over, I should get a new tablecloth or a centerpiece or at least flowers for the table. Christmas is coming. I should get this and this and this. What I've learned is that those things don't matter, but they do add up. It's the way I end up spending $200 at the store when I go in for three things.

When I think of 50 percent of people living on seven dollars a day, I don't want all my money to go to stuff. I want it to go to things that matter. At the end of my life, I want to know that I stewarded well what God gave to me, and to steward well includes giving generously both to God and man.

Recently I went through the book of Malachi on my podcast, *Little Things*. It is the last book of the Old Testament. In it, God confronts the people about what they were saying about him and how they were treating him. Look at what God told his people about giving offerings to him:

> **"You are under a curse—your whole nation—because you are robbing me. Bring the whole tithe into the storehouse, that there may be food in my house. Test me in this," says the Lord Almighty, "and see if I will not throw open the floodgates of heaven and pour out so much blessing that there will not be room enough to store it. I will prevent pests from devouring your crops, and the vines in your fields will not drop their fruit before it is ripe," says the Lord Almighty. "Then all the nations will call you blessed, for yours will be a delightful land," says the Lord Almighty.** (3:9–12)

A tithe is a tenth. Moses commanded the people to give a tenth of their crops to the Lord to support the work of the Levites and the priests, because they didn't have an inheritance among the people. They were to be provided for through the people's offerings.

God said the people of Malachi's day were cursed because they were robbing God by not giving him his due.

Withholding offerings from God would be akin to an employer withholding the wages from an employee who earned the wage. God wanted his share. The irony was that in the process of trying to save a little by not giving it to God, they were keeping themselves from receiving the blessing God was willing and wanting to give them.

Luke 6:38 says:

> **"Give, and it will be given to you. A good measure, pressed down, shaken together and running over, will be poured into your lap. For with the measure you use, it will be measured to you."**

When we hold on to our things, we lose far more than we gain. Charles Dickens illustrated this concept in his famous novella *A Christmas Carol.* Ebenezer Scrooge stored up all he had and refused to share anything with anyone. He wouldn't give to charity on Christmas Eve. He didn't give his employee enough to get help for his son who was gravely ill. But as the Ghost of Christmas Yet to Come showed his life ebbing to a close, he realized he would die lonely and no one would mourn his passing. All the money he had gathered would do him no good in his death.

Conversely, Proverbs 11:25 says, **"A generous person will prosper; whoever refreshes others will be refreshed."** There's more than one way to be refreshed. The person of means may not need someone to buy them lunch, but it is refreshing indeed to be a person whom people enjoy sharing life with.

If those passages are true, and they are, you and I aren't doing ourselves any favors when we spend all we get on ourselves. When the money flies away on trifles or even the bigger purchases like cars and couches and whatever else, it's all too common to get to the end of the month and find there's nothing left to give to God or anyone else.

That's why the apostle Paul said, **"On the first day of every week, each one of you should set aside a sum of money in keeping with your income, saving it up, so that when I come no collections will have to be made"** (1 Corinthians 16:2). His point: Decide first what you will give, and set it aside. If you don't, you will likely spend all you have and won't have anything to give. Make generosity a priority, not an afterthought.

Make generosity a priority.

A common temptation is to assume if you give your money away, you won't have enough for yourself. God's promise in Malachi chapter 3 assures that just isn't the case. When you make him a priority, you will have all you need and more. David said as much in Psalm 37:25: **"I was young and now I am old, yet I have never seen the righteous forsaken or their children begging bread."**

That doesn't mean you should give frivolously beyond what you can or that you shouldn't save. Being good stewards of what God gives you includes both giving and being a responsible saver. But too many of us live in a state of perpetually spending all we have and sometimes more than what we have, leaving nothing to give.

You might think the little you have to give is inconsequential and the church, charities, and ministries wouldn't care about or miss small gifts. Nothing is further from the truth. If you're a person of little means, give a little.

Do you know the Bible account of Jesus sitting across from where the people were giving their offerings? Some people put in large amounts of money. But what impressed Jesus were not the clangings of a whole bunch of coins being dropped but rather when he heard a poor widow put in two small coins. He said: **"Truly I tell you, this poor widow has put more into the treasury than all the others. They all gave out of their wealth; but she, out of her poverty, put in everything—all she had to live on"** (Mark 12:43,44).

The note in my study Bible directs me to 2 Corinthians 8:12: **"For if the willingness is there, the gift is acceptable according to what one has, not according to what one does not have."**

God doesn't expect you to give what you don't have to give. He judges your motives and your willingness to part with some.

Why does this matter?

Jesus said, **"You cannot serve both God and money"** (Matthew 6:24). When you hold on to your money with clenched fists, you refuse to trust that God will keep his promise to provide.

There are plenty of places in Scripture where God provided for his people in miraculous ways. God fed his people manna in the desert. The prophet Elijah was fed by ravens until God directed him to go to a widow whose flour and oil did not dry up. Consider 2 Kings 4:1–7:

> **The wife of a man from the company of the prophets cried out to Elisha, "Your servant my husband is dead, and you know that he revered the Lord. But now his creditor is coming to take my two boys as his slaves."**
>
> **Elisha replied to her, "How can I help you? Tell me, what do you have in your house?"**
>
> **"Your servant has nothing there at all," she said, "except a small jar of olive oil."**
>
> **Elisha said, "Go around and ask all your neighbors for empty jars. Don't ask for just a few. Then go inside and shut the door behind you and your sons. Pour oil into all the jars, and as each is filled, put it to one side."**
>
> **She left him and shut the door behind her and her sons. They brought the jars to her and she kept pouring. When all the jars were full, she said to her son, "Bring me another one."**
>
> **But he replied, "There is not a jar left." Then the oil stopped flowing.**

> **She went and told the man of God, and he said, "Go, sell the oil and pay your debts. You and your sons can live on what is left."**

Elisha asked the widow, "What do you have?" That's a good question for you to ask too.

In June 2023, I signed up to take two classes at a Christian college. Those classes were sandwiched between my daughter's graduation and my son's wedding. As you can imagine, there were a lot of expenses happening simultaneously. At the same time, I wasn't picking up many hours at the nursing home where I was contracting because I had a lot going on.

For most of my children's growing up years, I enjoyed planting and expanding several perennial beds around our property. But with the kids getting older and moving on, I didn't want to weed my yard all summer.

As I was preparing for the graduation party, I noticed I had far too many plants, so I began to sell them on social media. I dug and divided and found more plants emerging and spreading. When it was all said and done, I sold enough plants to pay for my tuition that first session. I sold some more before the summer session in 2024.

God provided. When you go to him with your needs, and even your desires that are above and beyond your needs, he so often graciously gives what you ask. And sometimes he does that by opening your eyes to things you have but don't need.

The things most of us desire are things that can't be

bought like peace in our families, the love of others, and time with friends and family. When we have those things, we're filled in ways that money and things couldn't fill us.

So why do you and I worry we won't have enough? Our heavenly Father can richly supply all we need and more. Here's an example from Matthew 14:15–21:

> **As evening approached, the disciples came to him and said, "This is a remote place, and it's already getting late. Send the crowds away, so they can go to the villages and buy themselves some food."**
>
> **Jesus replied, "They do not need to go away. You give them something to eat."**
>
> **"We have here only five loaves of bread and two fish," they answered.**
>
> **"Bring them here to me," he said. And he directed the people to sit down on the grass. Taking the five loaves and the two fish and looking up to heaven, he gave thanks and broke the loaves. Then he gave them to the disciples, and the disciples gave them to the people. They all ate and were satisfied, and the disciples picked up twelve basketfuls of broken pieces that were left over. The number of those who ate was about five thousand men, besides women and children.**

Jesus took the little that his disciples found and multiplied it into more than enough. God's multiplication provides provision beyond our expectations. The apostle Paul put it this way: **"Now to him who is able to do immeasurably more than all we ask or imagine, according to his power that is at work within us, to him be glory in the church and in Christ Jesus throughout all generations, for ever and ever! Amen"** (Ephesians 3:20,21). God is able to do more than we ask, more than we imagine, and more than we can measure.

If we're wise, we'd ask for more of the things that matter, such as more faith, more opportunities to share his Word, more men and women on the front lines doing kingdom work, more open doors for the gospel to spread, more Christ-centered communication to reach searching hearts, more families worshiping together, more churches reaching out to their communities, more, more, abundantly more!

Notice more the ways God abundantly blesses you day after day after day. What price would you put on being a child of God and heir to heavenly blessings? How much is a great marriage worth or having children who walk with God? How much would you pay to have godly friends whom you can laugh and cry with, who encourage you and pray for you?

I probably need another disclaimer as I wrap up this chapter. It's not a sin to have things, even wealth. In fact, God told the people through Jeremiah: **"Seek the peace and prosperity of the city to which I have carried you into exile. Pray to the LORD for it, because if it prospers, you too will prosper"** (29:7).

We want our cities, states, and nation to prosper. We want people to have good jobs so they can pay their bills and take their families on vacation. We want and should pray for peace and prosperity.

The problem is not the wealth. The problem occurs when we keep it all for us and refuse to be generous toward God and others. Look at Jesus' parable:

> **"The ground of a certain rich man yielded an abundant harvest. He thought to himself, 'What shall I do? I have no place to store my crops.'**
>
> **"Then he said, 'This is what I'll do. I will tear down my barns and build bigger ones, and there I will store my surplus grain. And I'll say to myself, "You have plenty of grain laid up for many years. Take life easy; eat, drink and be merry."'**
>
> **"But God said to him, 'You fool! This very night your life will be demanded from you. Then who will get what you have prepared for yourself?'**
>
> **"This is how it will be with whoever stores up things for themselves but is not rich toward God"** (Luke 12:16–21).

God blessed the man with a good harvest, but the man refused to acknowledge God by giving even a little back to him.

I'm so glad Jesus wasn't stingy in his love for us. Imagine if he came to earth and then decided he only wanted to give part of himself. Or what if when it came down to it, he decided the sacrifice was too much?

Instead, he suffered. Even as he was suffering, he prayed that God would forgive those who mocked and scorned him. After he rose, he sought out Peter, his dear friend who had denied knowing him only a few days before. He would have even forgiven Judas if Judas had come to him for forgiveness.

I'm so glad Jesus wasn't stingy in his love for us.

If you, like me, have been hanging on a little too tightly, this might be the reminder you need. You and I can't take it with us, but we can use it to do a lot of good before we go. Be confident that God will provide what you need.

WHAT DOES THIS MEAN FOR YOU?

1. To have a spirit of generosity is to go against everything you see on social media and TV. Day after day, you're bombarded with images of perfectly decorated houses; new, fresh clothes and haircuts; the latest gadgets and technology. With the finite amount of money you have, you might need to put blinders on to those things in order to be generous to God and others. How do you make that happen?

2. Make a list of how you'd like to use your money. Include the ministries and charities you'd like to support.

3. Since cleaning out other people's houses, I keep finding things around my house that I don't use or don't even like anymore. I bought a lot of those things. At the time they seemed like good ideas, but now they're just in my way. A big part of change is self-awareness, realizing when you're doing things that aren't serving you well in order that you choose differently in the future. What is the "more" you really crave? Is it more time with your spouse or children, more friends, more peace, a closer walk with God?

4. What steps can you take to ensure your money goes where you want it to go instead of being used on frivolous things while simultaneously pursuing the things you really desire?

CHAPTER 10

Confident Your Worry Isn't Helping the Situation

I legit hate worry. (Maybe you label it anxiety.) I despise it, mostly because it has stolen way too many otherwise perfect days. Worry is the most useless of emotions, and yet it is so easy to fall into. It is living in the realm of "what if" instead of dealing with whatever is at hand today and letting whatever tomorrow brings be a tomorrow problem.

Worry, anxiety, and fret are rooted in fear. They are the opposite of faith. God knew it would be a struggle for many people, so he gave the idea of worry, anxiety, fret, and fear a lot of real estate in the Bible. Over and over and over he says, "Do not worry. Do not be afraid. Do not fret. Fear not!"

The people God chose to put in the Bible weren't superhuman. They struggled with fear. Twice in the book of Genesis, Abraham feared for his life when going to a foreign land. His wife Sarah was very beautiful, and he feared the rulers would kill him and take Sarah. Both times Abraham lied and said Sarah was his sister, resulting in his wife being put in a heathen king's harem. Both times God worked on Sarah's behalf, despite Abraham.

God appointed a man named Gideon to rescue Israel from a vast army. Gideon needed continual reassurance that he was the one to do what God told him to do. (You can read his account in the Old Testament book of Judges chapter 6.)

In the book of Esther, God used Esther's courage to rescue his people. Esther did not volunteer to go to Xerxes to speak on behalf of her people. She had to be convinced!

Hebrews chapter 11 is known lovingly as the faith chapter in the Bible. It recalls the accounts of people in the Old Testament who did extraordinary things in faith.

Courage is not the absence of fear or worry.

Faith motivated Noah to believe God when he was told to build an ark. Think of how crazy he would have looked building a boat over 500 feet long!

Courage is not the absence of fear or worry. It is acting in spite of fear or through suffering or pain. It's keeping your eyes on God, even when the circumstances don't give you reason for hope.

Last summer I spent some time studying Psalm 119. It's the longest chapter in the Bible. The author chose to follow God and developed a deep love and admiration for God's ways, despite opposition. Verse 165 says, **"Great peace belongs to those who love your law, and nothing can make them stumble."**

I wrote that verse out on a piece of paper and keep it on my desk now. When the Bible speaks of peace, it is not the absence of turmoil. It is complete security knowing that God is in control; nothing takes him by surprise.

The more I read the Bible, the more convinced I am that worry is pointless. What is your greatest fear? Do you think God doesn't see you or your situation? He gives his assurance over and over that he does! Look at these passages:

- Psalm 34:15: **"The eyes of the Lord are on the righteous, and his ears are attentive to their cry."**
- Psalm 139:1–4: **"You have searched me, Lord, and you know me. You know when I sit and when I rise; you perceive my thoughts from afar. You discern my going out and my lying down; you are familiar with all my ways. Before a word is on my tongue you, Lord, know it completely."**
- Hebrews 4:13: **"Nothing in all creation is hidden from God's sight. Everything is uncovered and laid bare before the eyes of him to whom we must give account."**

Do you doubt God will act on your behalf? Isaiah 30:19 says: **"You will weep no more. How gracious he will be when you cry for help! As soon as he hears, he will answer you."**

Something will be given. It may be the strength you need to endure or patience to suffer well. He may send an angel to bring you to heaven, but you can know your prayers will be answered.

Are you worried that God doesn't know what is best? He knows better than you do. You and I are limited to our perspective and what we see. He knows motives and the truth of what people are thinking, and he knows the future.

Do you fret because something bad might happen? You can be sure it will. Jesus said you will have trouble (John 16:33). It's an absolute certainty that something will kill you. If not disease, then old age or an accident. God will take you to heaven. You will die, and so will your loved ones. God does not guarantee a long life nor that things will go your way. But Romans 8:28 gives absolute certainty that whatever you face or go through will have a purpose. There will be good. God will work on your behalf.

In the Old Testament, God often reminded the people that he was the God who brought them out of Egypt. One generation experienced it, the next heard about it from the people who had lived through it, but God made a point to remind the generations after that. He told them to celebrate the Passover every year. Why was it so important?

The people had been slaves in Egypt. They could do nothing to free themselves. Moses was a great prophet, but even he couldn't convince Pharaoh to let the people go. God sent the plagues, which were signs that should have convinced Pharaoh and all of Egypt who he was. But they didn't.

Finally, God sent an angel who killed every firstborn in Egypt. Then and only then were the Israelites allowed to leave. The Israelites were spared because they put the blood of a spotless lamb on their doorframes. The angel passed over their homes and spared their firstborns. For them to celebrate this every year was a way for God to remind them who he was. He was the only one who could save them from the hopelessness of their situation.

Everything pointed ahead to a time when Jesus would save them from the hopeless situation all mankind faces. We couldn't free ourselves from the slavery of sin. Only Jesus' blood could spare us from the devastation of death. We will still die, but when we do, we will be with God in heaven forever.

If Jesus did that, and he did at a great price—he left heaven where he was worshiped to experience the turmoil of life on earth and died the death we deserved in our place—why don't we think he would take care of us?

Account after account after account in the Bible shows God's faithfulness to his people. When they called to him, he answered. He delivered. God made promises, and those promises came true. He promised Abraham a son. He promised to bring the people of Israel out of Egypt. He promised to give them the land of Canaan. He promised to send a Messiah to save them from sin.

God made promises, and those promises came true.

He promises us that he will never leave us. He promises he will work all things for our good. He promises he will provide for us.

There have been times I couldn't see God's hand at work in my life. There were many times I didn't know how God would work things for good. There were even times I wondered if God really was with me because my life was a mess and I couldn't see what I wanted his presence to look like. But as I look back, he was at work. He continues to use what was meant to harm me for good. He was with me and provided for me in amazing and sometimes mysterious ways. He put the right people in my life at the right times.

And every time he did that in the past, he proved his faithfulness to me. That means I can trust him in the future, even when I can't see him and even when I don't understand his ways.

And when I trust God, it's harder to worry. Not that Satan and his army of angels aren't there taunting and tempting. They are. And sometimes I fall into worry, just as I fall into negative self-talk and doubting my worth in Christ. But more and more I recognize where the worry is coming from, just like I recognize where the negative self-talk is coming from. And sometimes I say out loud, *"You are faithful, God. You were with me in the past. You'll be with me in the future."* The more I say it, the more I believe it. And that's what God wants for you too.

That's why he said through the apostle Paul: **"Do not be anxious about anything, but in every situation, by prayer and petition, with thanksgiving, present your requests to God. And the peace of God, which transcends all understanding, will guard your hearts and your minds in Christ Jesus"** (Philippians 4:6,7).

God wants his peace to stand guard around your heart and mind. His peace is like a bouncer that doesn't let anxiety in. When you worry about what the doctor will say, his peace stands with arms folded, shaking his head. When trepidation about the myriad of issues facing your kids tries to sneak in, God's peace points you to 1 Peter 5:7: **"Cast all your anxiety on him because he cares for you."**

You are not meant to carry anxiety, trepidation, worry, and fear. God has big shoulders. He can carry all that you can't. He already knows the diagnosis. He already knows what your children will face, now and even after you're gone. That's why you can pray without ceasing. Pray prayers for God to carry your children until they are home. In my family, we pray to walk with God all the days of our lives. I don't just want my children to follow God now. I want them in heaven with me for eternity. I pray for God to put godly people in my children's lives always and for them to be the godly influences others need . . . not just now but with every breath.

God can carry all that you can't.

It took several painful seasons, but I've learned that only the Holy Spirit can change hearts and lives, and I can't convince anyone of my worth. Some people just won't like me. As much as I may want to see change, very often my words fall on deaf ears. My actions can be misconstrued. My efforts can go unnoticed and at times can even be mislabeled and misjudged. If I'm honest, those situations are the ones that bring the most worry and anxiety into my life.

For my husband, it was a job that no matter how hard he worked, it only continued to get more stressful. Try as he might, the demands continually went up with little support.

For both of us, the day finally came when our health, mental and physical, was suffering because of the situations. I needed to leave things I didn't want to leave. Steve needed a different job.

There are so many things that cause dread and anxiety in this world. But I have learned the importance of knowing and believing we have options. Too often we stay in situations hoping and praying for change instead of realizing the change we need is to get out of the situation. Full stop. Read that again.

If you are the object of your spouse's abuse and cower every night until he or she falls asleep, my guess is any time you are in the same room as that spouse, your anxiety is high. God doesn't expect you to stay there being abused. Look for the people who can help you find a way out.

If you have been living a life away from God and you find yourself envying the life you crave with a family and God, find a way to call home. Cry out to God. **"A broken and contrite heart you, God, will not despise"** (Psalm 51:17). If your parents are Christians, my guess is your return home would alleviate some of their anxiety.

I would have loved for the situations I was in to change, but the only change that occurred was from bad to worse. The same was true with Steve's job. And eventually I realized the anxiety I carried—for me about saying the next wrong thing to set someone off and for Steve walking into work every day knowing there was no way for him to do his job well—is a weight that makes every day a struggle until the situation changes.

When the situation changes, then the weight and anxiety are gone. That's not to say they're gone forever. There was a lot of anxiety every time I ran into one of the people who made my life hard. My body reacted when people unknowingly said things about not trying hard enough or walking away instead of working it out or about submitting to authority. I believe in submitting to authority. But I also believe it is an abuse of power to use the power you've been given as a club to beat down someone who points out flaws you don't want to address.

So often there aren't easy answers. Not everyone can leave a job, especially when they have 30 years in and they're at the top of the pay scale. Leaving would mean starting over. I get it. It can be complicated to leave the situation when children and money are wrapped up in it.

But difficult and complicated are not the same as impossible. In the Bible, Abraham's wife Sarah had a servant named Hagar. Hagar was involved in something complicated. It wasn't her idea to sleep with Abraham and get pregnant. It was Sarah's, and as soon as Hagar was pregnant, Sarah was jealous. When Sarah had a baby of her own 13 years later, Sarah convinced Abraham to send Hagar and her son, Ishmael, away. Here's what happened:

Early the next morning Abraham took some food and a skin of water and gave them to Hagar. He set them on her shoulders and then sent her off with the boy. She went on her way and wandered in the Desert of Beersheba.

When the water in the skin was gone, she put the boy under one of the bushes. Then she went off and sat down about a bowshot away, for she thought, "I cannot watch the boy die." And as she sat there, she began to sob.

God heard the boy crying, and the angel of God called to Hagar from heaven and said to her, "What is the matter, Hagar? Do not be afraid; God has heard the boy crying as he lies there. Lift the boy up and take him by the hand, for I will make him into a great nation."

Then God opened her eyes and she saw a well of water. So she went and filled the skin with water and gave the boy a drink.

God was with the boy as he grew up. He lived in the desert and became an archer. (Genesis 21:14–20)

Was Hagar's life complicated? Yes. Was it easy? No. Did God make a way? He did. And he will for you too. That's why you keep asking him to show you the way and to help, trusting that he will. For me, it was leaving. For you, it may be staying but with new boundaries or finding a place of peace even in that job or situation to shield you from the people who make you crazy.

God sees you and knows your limitations. But he is also a way-maker who can make a way where you never could.

WHAT DOES THIS MEAN FOR YOU?

1. What do you worry about most?

   Is it something that is in your power to change? If so, what do you need to do to get out of or change the situation?

   If you can't change it, it means it is something only God can change. Read Luke 18:1–8. Rather than worry, what course of action can change the situation?

2. Write out Matthew 16:23.

   This is a great response when you are spiraling into worry or fear. Say Jesus' words out loud as a declaration! You can be certain worry is not from God because he tells you so often not to fear. If it's not from God, then it's from the devil, the world, or your own thoughts. Whichever it is, it is not in your best interest, nor does it bring glory to God. Rather than fall into it, you can declare, *"Get behind me, Satan. You do not have in mind the things of God."* God's

Word assures you that God will be with you, will help you, will provide for you here and forever. Every time you do this, it will become easier to refuse to fall into worry and instead respond in faith.

CHAPTER 11

Confident You Don't Have to Be Your Own Worst Enemy Anymore

This chapter is for my friends who are like me. Perhaps you have an appetite for control, but you are realizing you can't do it all. In all truth, there's so little you can control. Let go. Let others help.

The biggest lesson I learned concerning control happened when I listened to Pastor Mike Novotny's *Time of Grace* series about the letters to the churches in the book of Revelation (*Jesus Judges Churches Too* series). Jesus would have been the perfect person to run the churches, but he didn't. He left. He went back to heaven and left the entire Christian church in the hands of sinful people who would mess up.

If Jesus left the church in the hands of sinners, there shouldn't be a whole lot that you can't hand over. Maybe you can do it better, but are you the only one who can do it? Is it what you are uniquely qualified to do, or do you need to loosen your grip a little for the sake of your sanity and the sanity of everyone who needs to live with you?

If you are a spouse, then you are the only wife or husband your spouse has. If you are a parent, you are the only mom or dad your child has. Those are roles you can't delegate. If I were to die tomorrow, there would be others to write books, other voices to create podcasts, other people to pray for the lost.

You do a terrible disservice to others when you hold on too tightly. As Jesus was ascending to heaven, he gave a command known as the Great Commission. His command was to make disciples of all nations. That means he wants you to do what he did. He trained his disciples and sent them out. He knew he couldn't go everywhere himself. And he knew he would only be on earth for a short time.

What a blessing if you approach life like you aren't going to be here forever. Far too often you and I aren't looking for replacements. We aren't equipping our fellow Christians to work in the kingdom. And we all suffer because of it.

The apostle Paul said, **"So Christ himself gave the apostles, the prophets, the evangelists, the pastors and teachers, to equip his people for works of service, so that the body of Christ may be built up until we all reach unity in the faith and in the knowledge of the Son of God and become mature, attaining to the whole measure of the fullness of Christ"** (Ephesians 4:11–13).

The apostles, prophets, evangelists, pastors, and teachers weren't to do all the work themselves. Their job was to equip the saints to work in the kingdom.

The same is true in our homes. As parents, our job is to teach our children to be independent, to be able to live without us, to bring up children who know Christ. Children learn as they participate in the work.

Maybe control isn't the thing that is capsizing your boat. Maybe you have let Satan and/or his minions get in your head. You thought you would be a spark of change in your church or at work or at the very least in your home. But here you are feeling like a failure.

"Who do you think you are?"

"You are so stupid."

"Of course it didn't work. When do you ever do anything right?"

Do any of those statements sound familiar? If they do, then it's time to get serious about taking back your mind.

The apostle Paul said, **"We demolish arguments and every pretention that sets itself up against the knowledge of God, and we take captive every thought to make it obedient to Christ"** (2 Corinthians 10:5).

Demolish means "to knock down, to overwhelmingly defeat." Pretension is a claim. In plain, simple English: Destroy every claim that is against God's nature or God's Word. Be aggressive, and take that thought captive. Don't be taken prisoner. You can control your thoughts, and you do it by knowing the truth of the Word of God.

"Who do you think you are?"

"Well, Satan, I know who I am. I'm a child of God, and my Father is the King of kings and Lord of the universe. He hears my every prayer. I am royalty, entitled to all the benefits and privileges of an heir."

"Are you stupid?"

"Nope. I've made plenty of bad decisions, but that doesn't make me stupid, just human."

"When do you ever get anything right?"

"A whole lot of times, that's when! I might do 101 things right all day without thinking about it. I read my Bible and changed the toilet paper roll (because I'm a responsible adult and that's the decent thing to do) and made coffee for my spouse. I emptied the lint trap and did the dishes and drove the speed limit. I refuse to focus on the one thing that didn't go well or that I messed up instead of remembering all that I did well to serve my family, spouse, and the Lord."

Your sinful nature and the devil and his army are good at put-downs. Several years ago, a friend taught me that when these thoughts appear, my job is to remember they are not from God. If they aren't from God, then they are from the army of evil, so you can tell them to go right back to hell where they belong.

Maybe you sabotage your days by constant negativity, gossip, and grumbling. Something happens or doesn't go as you want or someone doesn't perform the way you think they should, and you're on the phone reporting it to the first person who will listen. Do you know what you're doing to yourself when you respond that way? You are releasing cortisol, the stress hormone. You are literally stressing yourself out and telling your body everything is bad.

Instead of complaining, learn to give thanks. First Thessalonians 5:18 says, **"Give thanks in all circumstances; for this is God's will for you in Christ Jesus."** It's God's will that you thank him for everything. That load of laundry: give thanks. You have a washer, you have soap, you have a washing machine, and you have people you love in your family.

Give thanks for traffic. It means you have a car. When you feel sick, it's a reason to give thanks for all the days you've felt well. And thank God for all the conveniences you have available to you that generations past didn't have.

Giving thanks for everything will change your brain. You will start seeing the good more and notice even more good. Before long, you will be amazed at how happy you are and how little you care about things that don't go your way.

Giving thanks for everything will change your brain.

Another way to keep from being your own worst enemy is to set yourself up for success. A few years back, Pastor Mike Novotny wrote the book *What's Big Starts Small* based on the parable of the sower. In the parable Jesus told of a farmer who sowed seed. The seed landed on different types of soil. The plant that grew depended on the type of soil the seed landed on. In his explanation of the parable, Jesus said: **"The seed falling on good soil refers to someone who hears the word and understands it. This is**

the one who produces a crop, yielding a hundred, sixty or thirty times what was sown" (Matthew 13:23).

Both this parable and the parable of the bags of gold that is recorded in Matthew 25:14–30 talk about using what we've been given. Each of us has a certain amount of time, different spiritual gifts, a body, and potential.

I want to do the most good with the time that I have until God takes me to heaven. I want be as healthy as I can be and use the time God has given me wisely. It's easier for me to do that when I set myself up to succeed. Here's what I mean.

If I have healthy food in the fridge and cupboard, that is what I am most likely to eat. If I have the exercise mat where it's easy to access, I'll be more prone to getting my sit-ups and push-ups done. I make a point to walk with friends once or twice a week so my walks are a joy and not drudgery.

I make it hard to access my phone. I put it on silent, and put it away while working so I'm not tempted to pick it up or look at it.

If reading the Bible is a challenge for you, consider rewarding yourself for reading it. Make coffee so it's ready to pour once you've finished. Do prayers and family devotions before you watch an episode of that detective show. Whatever bad habit causes grief, make a change to make it harder to fail.

Laundry was always a struggle for me. I'd take things out of the dryer, put them in a laundry basket, and pretty soon I'd have four laundry baskets full of laundry to fold. I hated folding laundry and despised laundry baskets all over the house.

So I started folding the clothes right as they came out of the dryer. Everything got folded and put in piles, and the piles were delivered to everyone's rooms or put away in their closets. Now I never have laundry baskets full of clothes. In fact, I don't even use laundry baskets anymore! And even better, I don't have a laundry basket full of stray socks to match.

These are just a few of the little things that can make a big difference in the way we take care of our bodies, spend our time, and keep a house.

Don't be content to keep failing. Ask others what they've found that helps. One step in the right direction beats ten in the wrong direction.

And last and maybe most important, don't let failure keep you from trying again. Everyone fails. We try, we struggle, we adjust, and we do something different.

Thomas Edison is famously quoted as saying, "I have not failed 10,000 times—I've successfully found 10,000 ways that will not work." What a great way to reframe the situation.

So what if you failed yesterday? Fail forward today. What did you learn? Some of the greatest failures have been the impetus to the greatest successes. Dave Ramsey filed for bankruptcy before starting a company teaching people how to get out of debt. Joseph was in prison (through no fault of his own) before he became Pharaoh's right-hand man.

Don't stay down, and don't let anyone but God define your identity. Don't hold on to control while driving everyone around you away. Build people up. Encourage them.

Help them succeed, and enjoy their success with them. Keep growing and trying new things and being thankful for whatever each new day brings. Rely on God to help you. Be your own best friend instead of your worst enemy. A year from now, you could be in a whole different situation.

WHAT DOES THIS MEAN FOR YOU?

1. Sometimes we don't see the ways we sabotage our lives. Read Psalm 139:23,24. God sees it all and knows. How does this passage lead you to pray?

2. You have to become a warrior to confront the nonsense the devil and his evil army and your sinful self throw at you. The negative self-talk will paralyze you if you listen to it. You have to slay, demolish, destroy the negative voices over and over and over while reminding yourself of the truth: *"I am worthy. Jesus died for me. I do matter. God knows the number of hairs on my head. He cares about the birds, but he cares about me far, far more."* What lies have you been believing, and what is the truth of God's Word you will use to confront the lies?

3. Write down one change you are going to make to set yourself up to be more effective in God's kingdom. Maybe it's going to bed at 10 P.M. so you are sharper in the morning to serve your family or be less cranky at work. Maybe it's giving up soda and instead drinking lemon water to keep yourself hydrated and to cut the

sugar intake that leaves you groggy. What change will you make today?

4. We all need accountability partners. Who can you entrust to hold you accountable to make the change and to encourage you when you are stuck and still listening to the voices in your head?

CHAPTER 12

Confident You Are the One to Get the Job Done

It's easy to look at all the things that are wrong with the world and wonder who is going to make a change. Surely there are brilliant people who could come up with innovative ideas to advance life in a certain way. Someone somewhere could figure out how to turn slums into practical places with low-income housing that would be both sanitary and safe. Someone somewhere is creative enough to figure out a way to filter the contaminants from filthy rivers and turn them into usable drinking water. Someone must have an idea to address the homeless crisis or the drug problem or issues pertaining to social media and the mental health of young people.

But that's not you. I get it. For a minute, forget about out there. What about the problems right where you are?

I couldn't tell you the day or even the year, but I remember sitting on the couch one day next to my husband, Steve. Our four young kids were having one of those days when no one could get along, and the crabbiness and fighting were constant. Finally, Steve looked at me and said, "Well, I guess this is our mess to deal with."

As much as we hoped someone would sweep in and rescue us from the chaos of the situation, Steve was right. It was our mess, and we were the only ones who could change the situation.

Not every problem requires brilliance or an extra measure of creative potential. Sometimes it just requires willing hearts and open hands. And sometimes one person starting is all it takes to motivate others to help.

Maybe you don't have a small group Bible study at your church, yet you long for closer relationships and friends who hold you accountable. Reach out to your pastor and ask what needs to be done to make it happen. Maybe you don't feel qualified to teach the study. Could you host it at your house? Could you make a meal to bring to someone else's house, making it easier for people to come right after work?

Or maybe you notice the church property looks dilapidated. Contact your church president and find out what needs to be done to renovate it. Solicit some of the business owners from church to see if they would contribute. You might be surprised at how willing people are to get behind the project.

But maybe you aren't an idea person or an activator (someone who initiates action and is impatient for progress to be made). Maybe you are a worker bee. You'll happily pitch in when something needs to be done, but you don't usually come up with the idea. Fair enough. You don't have to go far to hear or see a need. The Sunday school superintendent is overwhelmed. Or the church flower calendar is blank, and no one has signed up to bring flowers to put on the altar. The homebound members aren't being visited. Send a card if you can't visit!

Instead of waiting for someone else to step up or step in, consider how you can be a part of the solution. When someone mentions they are overwhelmed because they have x, y, and z to do, take one of those things off their plate. Contribute in a small way.

God didn't intend for you to carry the world. Not every problem is your issue. There's a whole lot you can't do and can't change. But there are certain things you can and should do. First and foremost, if you are reading or listening to this book right now, I'm going to assume you are able to pray. The older I get, the more I realize the importance of doing so.

The apostle Paul reminds us, **"Our struggle is not against flesh and blood, but against the rulers, against the authorities, against the powers of this dark world and against the spiritual forces of evil in the heavenly realms"** (Ephesians 6:12). Your spouse, your boss, your children, your pastor, and everyone else are not the problem. The problem is the army of evil who incites and tempts and lures everyone they can into unholiness. (Which means they are at work on you too, inciting you to say or do the wrong thing and inciting you to react the wrong way.)

If prayer is not a normal part of your day, consider it the first and only thing worth changing in your life right now. Set aside five minutes in the morning or a few minutes at lunch, or make time after dinner. Any time is a good time to pray.

I'm not going to take up space in this chapter, but know there is a list of things to pray for at the end of this book on page 173. I don't know anyone who says they pray enough, so use those ideas as prayer prompts.

Any time is a good time to pray.

If you're not in a position to start a seemingly monumental task, be on the lookout to do what Mother Teresa called small things with great love. Seemingly insignificant things can often be the difference between a day going terrible and a day going well. Send a text or a card or take the time to call someone. Let the man or woman with a fidgety child go in front of you in line. Ask a widow to go to coffee, or sit with a person who takes care of their spouse. Let them tell you how hard the days can be.

If you are at a point that you could do something more, ask God what that more is. Keep your eyes open.

The apostle Paul told Timothy: **"Command those who are rich in this present world not to be arrogant nor to put their hope in wealth, which is so uncertain, but to put their hope in God, who richly provides us with everything for our enjoyment. Command them to do good, to be rich in good deeds, and to be generous and willing to share"** (1 Timothy 6:17,18).

John the Baptist's definition of excess was this: **"Anyone who has two shirts should share with the one who has none, and anyone who has food should do the same"** (Luke 3:11). If John the Baptist saw my closet or pantry or freezer, he'd probably ask why I haven't brought a warm meal or a fresh pair of socks or a sweater to a homeless person.

Can you imagine if we, the church, started doing that? Imagine making a meal, putting it in containers, and driving around your town to find someone in need. Imagine parking the car, getting out, and sitting with the person, finding out their name, praying for them, and reminding them of their worth in Christ.

Hebrews 13:16 says, **"And do not forget to do good and to share with others, for with such sacrifices God is pleased."** God is pleased when we take some of what we have and share it with people who need our help.

What might God be willing to do through you?

Judges chapter 3 introduces us to Ehud, a left-handed man who was sent to deliver tribute (annual payment) to the king of Moab. Somehow, he was able to get right up to the king and tell the king he had a secret message. When the king dismissed all his servants, Ehud plunged an 18-inch sword through the king's belly. Then Ehud locked the door and escaped, allowing enough time to escape, gather troops, and strike Moab, bringing freedom to Israel that lasted 80 years.

A note in one commentary on this Bible section is significant. It suggests that "either Ehud was born with a natural preference for his left hand, or he was handicapped.

The Hebrew expression for left-handedness is 'restricted as to the right hand.' Being merely left-handed would not have been sufficient cover for the stratagem Ehud used to approach King Eglon with a concealed weapon. We would not expect a healthy-looking person, right-or left-handed, to pass the Moabite bodyguards without a body check. No, the text leads us to believe that the Moabites let down their guard at Ehud's approach because he did not physically look the part of a dangerous fighter. We can almost hear the Moabites jeer as they looked at Ehud's useless right hand. 'How low have the "mighty men" of Israel sunk to have sent such a one!'"[17]

When it comes to what you can and can't do in God's kingdom, it is always about who God is, not who you are. Whether you are weak or strong, old or young, male or female, a citizen or immigrant is of no consequence to God. He is able to do **"immeasurably more than all we ask or imagine, according to his power that is at work within us"** (Ephesians 3:20).

Immeasurably more means it's too large, extensive, or extreme to measure. It's something bigger, wider, stronger, farther than you could imagine. Only God knows the reach your good works may have. That one person you build up and help out may go on to tell hundreds about Christ. The one child you teach may bring his or her whole family to know Christ. The prayers you pray today may yield exponential dividends in the future.

God has work for you to do right here and right now. You are the one. And there's lots to do.

WHAT DOES THIS MEAN FOR YOU?

1. Look at your situation right now. What issues drive you nuts in your neighborhood, at work, or at church? What can you do about them?

2. Read Romans 12:1–8. So often when we think about giving an offering to the Lord, we think about money. The apostle Paul challenges us to think about our lives! He tells us to use sober judgment. That is the ability to know what we're good at and what we're not good at. How will this help when it comes to doing what needs to be done?

3. Look again at the list of gifts in Romans 12:6–8. How has God gifted you to bless the church?

4. Paul doesn't just tell you what to do; he tells you how to do it. Look at the way you are to serve. How can you make sure you're serving with a right heart?

CHAPTER 13

Confident God Can See a Future You Can't Imagine

I get it. You aren't in a position to dream. You're stuck. You're putting one foot in front of the other.

A few months ago, I was speaking at a conference. When the conference was over, I talked to a woman for quite a while. Her husband of 40-plus years went to heaven a few months earlier after a 3-month illness. This woman said she could hardly get out of bed the first 3 weeks after his death. And then she had a realization that changed everything.

It would never have been enough. Even if her husband lived another 10 years, she wouldn't have been ready for him to die.

She decided to get a job. She had retired a year earlier and decided she didn't want to be alone every day. A few weeks later she started over.

Your journey from seeing things as never enough to

seeing God always provides enough is realizing God's ways are good even when they aren't your ways. His timing is right even when it's not your timing.

Nowhere in the Bible are we led to believe God has limited resources. In fact, we're told just the opposite. God is far bigger than we are capable of understanding. He brought the universe into existence with his word. God's love won't run out. That does not mean if you imagine it, you can do it. God isn't a genie, at your beck and call to give you whatever you desire.

His timing is right.

You have limitations. You have a finite supply of money. Your responsibilities hinder you from doing whatever you want whenever you want. You have a varying degree of health. There are, however, three things you can control:

1. Your time.
2. Your energy.
3. Your effort.

Every day you have 24 hours. What do you want to do with those hours? Subtract the amount of time you need for working, sleeping, commuting, getting ready, and taking care of household chores, and you might still be left with free time. Do you want to spend that in front of the TV or on your phone? Or with friends?

Energy is the strength and vitality required for a physical or mental activity. It is closely tied to your food/beverage intake, your age, and your overall health. If you consume sugary foods and drinks like I did for many years, you may experience a surge of energy followed by a pretty significant crash as your body works to bring your blood sugar down. Caffeine, energy drinks, sugar, protein, carbs, water intake as well as having the kind of job you have all play a role in the amount of energy you have to do what you want to do.

Effort means a vigorous or determined attempt. What could you do if you focused your effort on a specific task?

Twice in the last four years I saw how focusing time, energy, and effort could make a significant difference in my life and the lives of those around me. From 2020 to 2021, I was laid off from my job as an elderly companion, at the same time my church, where I was volunteering a lot, shut its doors. I suddenly had time and nowhere to go and nothing to do. So I started going through my house meticulously. I went through the storage areas and closets. I threw a lot away and donated what was left. I repainted and simplified our living areas.

As soon as it was warm enough, my husband and I did the same thing in our yard. We removed flowerbeds and planted grass in their place. We turned a wooded area of our yard into a firepit and garden. We started what has been a four year and still not finished process of beautifying problem areas in our yard. We stained the deck.

I'm not exaggerating when I say it changed our lives. We've hosted many get-togethers since then and have people over regularly to our house.

Every year I continue to make the upkeep in our house/ yard less work, because it's not important anymore. We love having a place for people to gather but want to spend minimal time maintaining our possessions.

The decision for me to go back to work in 2021 was in an effort to bring us to a place of financial freedom. Two years working as a traveling nursing assistant was a blessing that has impacted our family in significant ways.

Both of these things were a matter of pivoting. There was a lot I couldn't do in 2020. But instead of getting stuck in what couldn't be done, I focused on what could. The first part, the cleaning out part, didn't require any money.

It's easy to focus on what won't work without seeing what will. So much can be accomplished when you have an undivided heart and mind, a goal worth pursuing, a willingness to do what needs to be done, and God with you.

The opposite is also true. It's amazing how little will be accomplished when your efforts are scattered and you don't have a clearly defined goal to work toward.

If what you pray for or strive for and hope and work toward with all your heart is not according to God's will, you will not succeed. Solomon said as much in Psalm 127:1: **"Unless the Lord builds the house, the builders labor in vain. Unless the Lord watches over the city, the guards stand watch in vain."**

So, what is the desire of your heart, and how do you know if it aligns with God's desire for your life? You can start by asking yourself these questions: *"What is my motive for wanting this? Whom will it bless? How will this help me live differently to honor God?"*

You may think you have the perfect plan, but God may see something entirely different in your future.

I mentioned Joseph from the Bible earlier in this book. He was sold by his brothers and taken to Egypt. He couldn't have known what would come about when he was taken to Egypt. Esther wouldn't have known when she was orphaned what would happen in the years ahead. Ruth would have no way of knowing that her first husband would die, which would lead to a move that would someday bring her into the line of the Savior.

Joseph probably wanted to carry on his father's legacy in Canaan. Esther probably would have wanted an in-tact family. Ruth may have desired, possibly even prayed for, a family with her first husband. Saul, who became the apostle Paul, probably prayed God would bless his work destroying the new Christian church. As an upstanding Pharisee, he was convinced his work was God's will. Little did he know it wasn't, and God would turn him from a persecutor of the Christian church to a man who would spend the rest of his life being persecuted for the Christian church.

All this is to say that the prayer for all of us needs to be: *"Open the doors you would have me go through, and close the ones I shouldn't. Align my heart with yours, and give me kingdom opportunities!"*

So much of life is perspective. Our sinful selves tempt us to want more. But God knows that more often lets us down and brings more of all the wrong things. We think we'll get more money, but we get more struggle. We think we'll be respected, but we're scrutinized. We think people will like us, but in truth, they like what we can do for them.

The "more" we want is only found in Christ. Emptiness continues to devour until it is satisfied in God. Then and only then do we find the peace that passes all understanding. We go to God empty, and he fills us up. We offer nothing. He gives us more than we knew we needed.

Earlier this year, I did a 30-day challenge. Every day I answered three questions: What filled me with enthusiasm today? What drained my energy today? What did I learn about myself today?

It's amazing the patterns I found when I did this, and once I saw the patterns, I could decide what to keep and what needed to go.

I am absolutely confident about three things in regard to your future:

1. Changing your attitude can help you through any situation. If you, like the apostle Paul, learn to be content in any and every situation, life will be considerably better.
2. Second, if you understand that your greatest need is taken care of—that when you take your last breath, as a believer in Christ you will be ushered into heaven where all your needs will be met, every longing filled,

every pain erased—you will care far less about everything else.

3. God does not change. If you live to old age, your body will age, and there's a good chance you will see your share of friends and family meet their earthly demise. Even then, God will not leave. He will be a constant companion when and if you have no one else.

The apostle Paul said it this way: **"For I am convinced that neither death nor life, neither angels nor demons, neither the present nor the future, nor any powers, neither height nor depth, nor anything else in all creation, will be able to separate us from the love of God that is in Christ Jesus our Lord"** (Romans 8:38,39).

Whatever hardship comes your way is temporary and minimal. It might hurt. It might not be your choice. But if you continue to walk with God and believe he is working all things for your good—you can be confident that he is in control and has your best in mind—then you can know beyond a shadow of a doubt that what he has for you is good.

WHAT DOES THIS MEAN FOR YOU?

1. Write down the biggest desire you have.

2. Answer these three questions regarding your biggest desire:

What is my motive for wanting this?

Whom will it bless?

How will this help me live differently to honor God?

3. In what ways do you struggle with feeling empty? Your emptiness can only be satisfied in God. What will you do to get more God in your life? How will you read your Bible differently? What Bible study could you join? What podcasts or worship music can you start listening to?

4. A few days ago, I spent time with two of my best friends. We spent a good chunk of time talking about heaven and what we are looking forward to once we are there. What are you most looking forward to? (If you don't know much about what heaven will be like, google "What does the Bible say about heaven?" You will find an abundance of passages to inform you!)

Conclusion

This book, as I prefaced at the beginning, is not about finding a new confidence in yourself. It is, however, about coming to a place where you can be completely and totally confident in God and his ability to work in and through your life.

For years I struggled with the idea that I was not enough. It's so easy for you and me to fall into that trap if we're looking at success the way the world views success. If we don't look right, have the right credentials, wear the right size, know the right people, or achieve the right goals, do we even matter?

Thankfully, God doesn't view us by worldly standards. He sees us through Jesus, and because of that, he sees us as beloved children. Being super good doesn't earn us more favor, and those sins we fall into again and again don't disqualify us from grace.

When we think we're not enough, it's easy to sit on the sidelines and wait for someone better to come along. Christ in us makes us always enough. Once we realize that, it's hard to be content on the sidelines. We want to do as much in God's kingdom as possible as long as we can. Time is short, and people need to know Jesus.

I don't know what has been a stumbling block to you or which lies Satan and his army whisper in your ear. But this book represents significant growth in my life. The topics covered represent a change in perspective.

Doors you wanted to open will close. People will let you down. You will at times run out of strength. Sometimes the "more" you were expecting turns out to be significantly less.

But when you know who God is and when you know who you are, those things don't matter as much as they once did. Your Father is the King of kings. He's crazy about you and hears every prayer. He knows your needs, and he's working on your behalf.

I wish that meant life would be easy. It isn't, and it won't be. But God doesn't leave you unequipped or ill-prepared. He makes sure you have everything you need to face whatever you face in each season.

And trust me when I say, it's enough.

Prayer Prompts

1. Pray for your church, that it would be a place where the gospel is freely proclaimed and where people come to find healing and strength. Pray that many would come through the doors and find the peace they are looking for. Pray for your pastor.

2. Pray for your family. Pray that those you love would walk with God and prioritize their relationship with him. Pray that God keeps them close all the days of their lives and brings them safely to their eternal dwelling. Pray that God doesn't allow the world and all its treasures to make them feel a false sense of security but that your family builds their foundation on the sure and lasting hope they have in Christ.

3. Pray the same for your friends and their families.

4. Pray for the straying, that God would use all means necessary to bring them back to the fold.

5. Pray for our nation, that godly rulers would be raised up to lead with integrity and truth.

6. Pray for your city and your neighborhood and for Christians around the world.

7. Pray for the people doing mission work, that God would open doors for the gospel message to spread and that the Holy Spirit would open hearts so it lands on fertile soil and grows.

8. Pray for the Christians being persecuted in other countries—that the gospel would continue to spread through them and that God would give them everything they need to get through each day. And, if I may be so bold, pray that God uses the messages of Time of Grace to reach searching hearts and through the Holy Spirit and the Word people come to know Jesus as their Savior.

9. Pray, always pray. Continue to pray. Never tire of praying. **"Pray without ceasing"** (1 Thessalonians 5:17 ESV). **"And pray in the Spirit on all occasions with all kinds of prayers and requests. With this in mind, be alert and always keep on praying for all the Lord's people"** (Ephesians 6:18). On *all* occasions with *all* kinds of prayers, *always*, for *all*.

10. Be alert. Notice when someone seems flustered. Notice when people are lonely or struggling and bring them to the throne of God. And as you notice and pray for them,

ask God to show you how you may be the answer to that prayer. Can you bring that older woman to an evening service at church or to a Bible study? Could you take a meal to the young mom so she gets a break for one night?

11. You have a problem? Pray. They have a problem? Pray. You see an issue? Pray.

Notes

1. *Evangelical Heritage Version Study Bible* (Milwaukee: Northwestern Publishing House, 2019), 378.
2. *Concordia Self-Study Bible* (Grand Rapids, MI: Zondervan Publishing House, 1984), 938.
3. Paul Wendland, 2 *Chronicles*, of The People's Bible series (Milwaukee: Northwestern Publishing House, 2002), 191.
4. *Concordia Self-Study Bible*, 641.
5. *Concordia Self-Study Bible*, 1511.
6. *Concordia Self-Study Bible*, 1511.
7. WELS Spiritual Gifts Discovery Tool, https://wels.net/wp-content/uploads/sgt/. Some of the information used, including the definitions of *spiritual gifts*, came from Professor David Valleskey, *Gifted to Serve* (Milwaukee: Northwestern Publishing House, 1983).
8. Bryant Wood, "The Walls of Jericho," Answers in Genesis, originally published March 1999, https://answersingenesis.org/archaeology/the-walls-of-jericho/.
9. *Evangelical Heritage Version Study Bible*, 1557.
10. *Concordia Self-Study Bible*, 1458.
11. *Concordia Self-Study Bible*, 1729.
12. *Concordia Self-Study Bible*, 720.

13. *Evangelical Heritage Version Study Bible,* 713.

14. *Concordia Self-Study Bible*, 1881.

15. John Jeske, *Genesis*, of The People's Bible series (Milwaukee: Northwestern Publishing House, 2001), 183.

16. "Overview," Understanding Poverty, World Bank Group, accessed November 21, 2024, https://www.worldbank
.org/en/topic/poverty/overview.

17. John Lawrenz, *Judges, Ruth*, of The Peoples Bible series (Milwaukee: Northwestern Publishing House, 2001), 50.

About the Author

Amber Albee Swenson has authored several books and is a regular blogger and podcaster for Time of Grace. Mostly she's amazed at God's goodness, awed by his wisdom and desire to grow her, and continually stretched by his calling in her life. For more details about her ministry, go to amberalbeeswenson.com. Listen to Amber's podcast, *Little Things*, at timeofgrace.org or on Spotify, Apple Podcasts, and many other podcasting platforms or by scanning this code:

Other Books by Amber

You Can Trust God When Life Hurts

Soul Care: Nurturing Your Spiritual Wellness

Chosen for More: Just as You Are

FIND THESE BOOKS AND MORE BY SCANNING THE CODE OR VISITING TIMEOFGRACE.STORE.

About Time of Grace

The mission of Time of Grace is to point people to what matters most: Jesus. Using a variety of media (television, radio, podcasts, print publications, and digital), Time of Grace teaches tough topics in an approachable and relatable way, accessible in multiple languages, making the Bible clear and understandable for those who need encouragement in their walks of faith and for those who don't yet know Jesus at all.

TO DISCOVER MORE, PLEASE VISIT
TIMEOFGRACE.ORG OR SCAN THIS CODE:

Help share God's message of grace!

Every gift you give helps Time of Grace reach people around the world with the good news of Jesus. Your generosity and prayer support take the gospel of grace to others through our ministry outreach and help them experience a satisfied life as they see God all around them.

GIVE TODAY AT TIMEOFGRACE.ORG/GIVE,
BY CALLING 800.661.3311,
OR BY SCANNING THE CODE BELOW.

THANK YOU!